THE BRIGHT STAR IN THE PRESENT PRO:

THE UNIVERSITY OF CHE
1839–2015

IAN DUNN

TRAINING COLLEGE, CHESTER.
Taken from the City Walls.

University of Chester Press

2015

Published by
University of Chester Press
Parkgate Road
Chester CH1 4BJ

First Published 2005
2nd Edition 2008
3rd Edition 2012
4th Edition 2015

Printed and bound in the UK by
CDP Print Management Limited

Designed by the
Learning and Information Services Graphics Team,
University of Chester

© Ian Dunn and the University of Chester, 2005, 2008, 2012, 2015

All Rights Reserved
No part of this publication may be reproduced, stored in a retrieval system or transmitted in any form or
by any means without the prior permission of the copyright owner, other than as permitted by current
UK copyright legislation or under the terms and conditions of a recognised copyright licensing scheme

A catalogue record for this book is available from the British Library

ISBN 978-1-908258-26-7

Contents

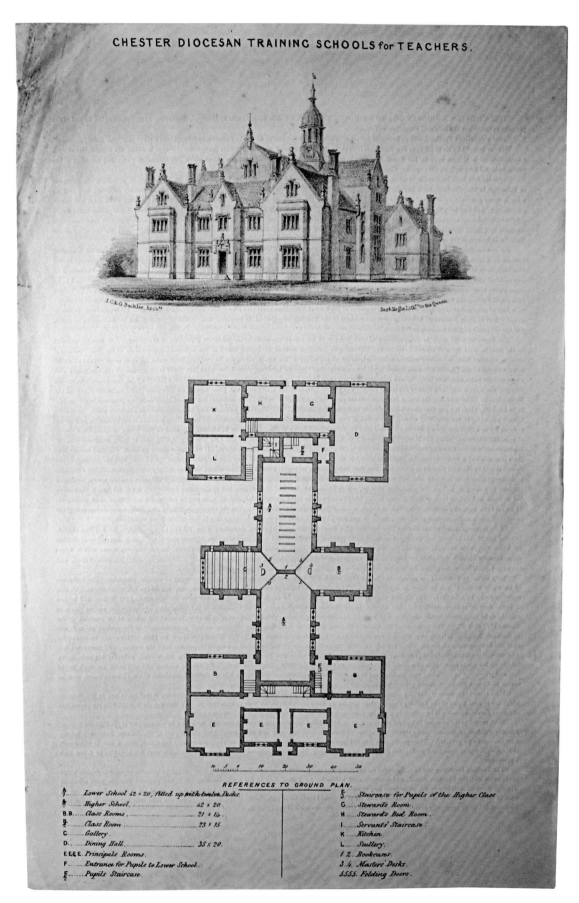

J.C.&G. Bucklers, Arch.ts   Day & Haghe, Lith.rs to the Queen

REFERENCES TO GROUND PLAN.

A .... Lower School 42 × 20, fitted up with twelve Desks.
B .... Higher School, ... 42 × 20
B.B. .... Class Rooms , ... 21 × 14.
C .... Class Room .... 23 × 15
C .... Gallery .
D .... Dining Hall .... 35 × 20.
E E E E. Principals Rooms .
F .... Entrance for Pupils to Lower School .
G .... Pupils Staircase .

G .... Staircase for Pupils of the Higher Class .
G .... Steward's Room .
H .... Steward's Bed Room .
I .... Servants' Staircase .
K .... Kitchen .
L .... Scullery .
1. 2. Bookcases .
3. 4. Masters' Desks .
5555. Folding Doors .

Above: J.C. and G. Bucklers' original designs for the new College buildings, 1841

FOREWORD

By the Vice-Chancellor and Principal of the University of Chester

Ten eventful years have now passed since the first edition of this book was commissioned in 2005 to celebrate the transition of Chester College into the University of Chester. Two further editions since then, and now a fourth, are but one indicator of the rapid and dramatic pace of development and expansion of this venerable institution since it took its rightful place amongst the distinguished list of English universities.

The Foreword I wrote to that first edition still has a relevance and resonance, speaking of traditions and values, hopes and expectations which have underpinned our development. They have happily been borne out by the story now told and it is therefore reprinted in full as a tribute to the decade of work of staff and students past and present and the high standards they have maintained. It also serves as an eloquent reminder of the memorable events of 2005 which have given such a solid base to education and to the intellectual, cultural and economic health of our region, a basis from which we now reach out nationally and internationally. Our balance of academic courses, 'traditional', innovative and vocational has been maintained and manifestly vindicated throughout a remarkable era in the history of the University.

This book marks the culmination of our celebrations of the 10th anniversary of the University and 175th of our institution. In thanking Ian Dunn, I am again proud to be able to record that our 'star' is still so conspicuously in the ascendant.

T.J. Wheeler

Canon Professor T.J. Wheeler DL

FOREWORD
to the first edition, 2005

By the Vice-Chancellor and Principal of the University of Chester

'One of the bright stars in the present prospect' was the phrase coined by Bishop Sumner to describe his newly established Chester College in 1844 and it provides a wonderfully apt sentiment today, as the institution enters into its most exciting phase as the University of Chester.

The continuities and connections to be found in our long history are striking. The regional importance of the new University has never been greater yet, even back in 1839, Chester College was the lynch-pin of Sumner's education strategy for his enormous diocese which covered most of the North West of England. The Warrington Campus is one of our most recent additions, which adds strength and depth to what the University can offer, and the part played by Warrington in the birth of the College can therefore only strike us with renewed significance. Similarly, from what we know of him, the first Principal, Arthur Rigg, would be delighted by the emphasis we now place on the vocational element of our courses and the employability of our students.

This book could as easily have been called *Principals and Principles*. The successive eras of the eleven Principals to date have all marked distinct phases, through trials and triumphs, and all have left their mark either on the culture and development of the institution or by the addition of buildings and new facilities. Yet each has maintained and found inspiration in the Christian ethic on which the College was founded. The support and involvement of the Bishop of Chester and the Dean of Chester Cathedral is as strong now as it was then and I am proud to have been appointed a lay canon of the Cathedral.

This book is a story of innovation, enterprise and adaptability and also, in recent times, one of astounding growth. It is scarcely believable that, in 1953, the total number of academic staff still amounted to no more than a dozen. There were no women students until 1961; women now account for two-thirds of our current student complement of 11,500. We began back in 1840 with 10 students in a small, and by all accounts gloomy, house in Nicholas Street, Chester. We now have two campuses in Chester and Warrington with the most up to date facilities to attract the students of the 21st century and a body of first class staff to guide and enlighten them; with a much lighter touch, let it be said, that the almost monastic regime of my Victorian predecessors.

These words and images, brought together for the first time so ably by Ian and Diana Dunn, commemorate a turning point in our history and a new University with long-established and sound traditions and values. A bright star indeed, now burning even more brightly in the present prospect.

J.J. Wheeler

Canon Professor T.J. Wheeler DL

Introduction

The University of Chester has a long and distinguished history. It is one of the oldest institutions of higher education in the country, pre-dating most universities; all, in fact, except Oxford, Cambridge, Durham and London. At the time that Chester College was founded for the training of teachers, there was nothing of equivalent breadth of conception or scope in England. The College therefore holds a unique place in the history of higher education, as the first institution in England set up to train teachers on anything resembling a modern method. It must be remembered that the trained schoolmaster was, in 1839, a complete innovation and a new sort of figure in society. The circumstances of the foundation were trail-blazing, the intentions noble, and the journey towards the achievement of university status must be regarded as a triumph. The intervening decades include many lesser triumphs over adversity, including difficulties imposed by two World Wars and threats to the College's very existence from the changes and chances of demography and national educational policy. The history of the institution which has become the University of Chester may be characterised as one of astonishing versatility and adroit adaptation to changing needs in the service it has rendered to education in England and beyond.

The social conditions and philanthropic moral climate which led to the setting up of the College carry us further back even than the accepted Foundation date of 1839. It is easy to forget that all six Founders and the first Principal spent their childhoods or early youth under the rule of the Prince Regent (later George IV), and four of them were born before the end of the 18th century. The England in which the College was created was as far removed from our own time in its social character as the world of the first Elizabeth was from the staff and students of the 1840s. The state took little or no part in the education of the people and, on the whole, felt no sense of responsibility for it. The provision of schools was left to the churches and to private enterprises or public charity. In the rapidly growing industrial towns and cities of the North West, all of which lay in the vast Diocese of Chester, around 40% of children grew up without educational instruction of any kind. Ashton-under-Lyne, for example, with a population of around 12,000, had not a single infant or day school and, as Bishop Sumner himself was to observe, in the town of Blackburn, in the year in which Queen Victoria came to the throne, only one in five children received any schooling. Even where schools existed in these regions, the vast majority of teachers had received no instruction whatever in the art of teaching. The proportion of the population who had, or could hope for, a college, let alone a university, education was very small indeed.

Chester itself was a modest cathedral city with a population of under 25,000. By 1840, its traditional economy had withered away and it was dependent on its role as a retailing, social and administrative centre. It had none of the wealthy manufacturers and capitalists of Liverpool, Manchester and other Northern towns, nor did it have a sizeable skilled working class. Except to the east, there were no substantial suburbs; in general, the city had not spread far beyond its celebrated medieval walls. Then, as now, the skyline was dominated by the Cathedral. The same local newspapers which advertised the meeting at which the Foundation of the College took place also carried advertisements for the mail and stage coaches which set out from the White Lion in Northgate Street. Chester was the centre from which the Bishop administered his unwieldy diocese, stretching from the Staffordshire border in the south to Kendal and Cockermouth in the Lake District and beyond, taking in large swathes of Cumbria and the whole of Lancashire, with its teeming manufacturing population. It was still a garrison town, the ancient centre of county government and the courts of law. It should not be forgotten that the late 1830s and the early 1840s were a period of frightening social unrest, and the 'Chartist riots' were witnessed with growing alarm in South Lancashire and North Cheshire especially.

Yet it was also an era of progressive thinking and reform. Social and moral consciences were stirring on a scale hitherto not seen in England; in Chester and the wider diocese, there was a body of men ready to take practical and effective action for the advancement of education for all.

The Founders

Few institutions of higher education can boast so distinguished an array of Founders. They were: **John Bird Sumner**, Bishop of Chester and later Archbishop of Canterbury; **Henry Raikes**, Sumner's lifelong friend, Chancellor of the Diocese of Chester, philanthropist and antiquarian; **James Slade**, Canon of Chester and Vicar of Bolton for almost 40 years, and one of the best known social reformers in the northern heartland; **The Hon. Horatio Powys**, Rector of Warrington and Rural Dean of Cheshire, later Bishop of Sodor and Man; **Lord Edward George Geoffrey Smith Stanley**, later 14th Earl of Derby, Chancellor of the University of Oxford, Knight of the Garter and three times Prime Minister; and, most distinguished of all, the **Rt Hon. William Ewart Gladstone**, then Vice-President of the Board of Trade and Privy Councillor, later Prime Minister on four separate occasions.

All these men were motivated by a high moral purpose and a sense of duty to improve the lot of the working population. They were united by a firm belief that the key to social improvement lay in education, that one of the principal obstacles to popular education was the lack of trained teachers and, with a view to meeting the spiritual as well as the earthly needs of the people, that education was best achieved under the auspices of the Established Church.

John Bird Sumner (1780–1862)

Sumner was educated at Eton and at King's College, Cambridge, where he achieved great academic distinction, winning the Hulsean Divinity Prize in 1802 and becoming a Fellow. Here, Raikes became a close friend. Returning to Eton as an assistant master ('the most popular of tutors'), he spent much of his spare time visiting the sick and the poor. He was elected a Fellow of Eton in 1817 and became a Canon of Durham in 1820. On the nomination of the Duke of Wellington, he was consecrated Bishop of Chester in September 1828.

His 19 years at Chester were acclaimed as a model of leadership, pastoral care and clear-sighted policy. Most reforming causes received his support, such as the repeal of the Corn Laws and Catholic Emancipation, and he voted for the great Reform Bill of 1832 and the new Poor Law Bill of 1834. He was one of the most prolific authors among bishops, producing over 40 books during his lifetime.

His strategy for the Diocese ('a poorly endowed, monstrously large and unmanageable unit') was the provision of additional church accommodation, especially for the poor; encouragement and support for the clergy; use of lay visitors; and promotion of education. He was convinced that, unless children grew up to be able to read and write, they could have no hope of improving their social or spiritual well-being. For Sumner, Christianity had to be the foundation underpinning all other aspects of education, and he considered that the crucial years 'for instructing the mind and forming the character' were from 10 to 15 years of age. He made education the central theme of his *Charge* to the Diocesan Clergy in 1838. In addition to promoting the building of new day schools, he also encouraged the development of Sunday Schools and evening classes. During his period at Chester, 233 new churches were built with accommodation for 194,745 people; the number of clergy was increased by 361 and 671 new day schools were erected. Yet his biographer Nigel Scotland says, 'The jewel in the crown of Sumner's educational strategy was to be his major role in the founding of Chester College'. He had a clear vision that good teachers would result in more and larger schools because, 'when parents realised there were good teachers in National schools, they would be prepared to pay a little for their children's education'. In his 1844 *Charge* to the Chester Diocese, he wrote, 'I believe we have taken the right step in applying ourselves to the education of masters in preparation for the education of our children. And I look to the Training College now happily established at Chester and able to send forth its thirty masters annually ... as one of the bright stars in the present prospect'.

In 1848, Sumner became Archbishop of Canterbury; to the delight, it is reported by his biographer, of Queen Victoria.

Henry Raikes (1782–1854)

Raikes was the nephew of the celebrated Robert Raikes, founder of the Sunday School Movement. He was educated at Eton and at St John's College, Cambridge. In 1828 he became examining chaplain to his university friend, Bishop Sumner, and in 1830 was appointed Chancellor of the Diocese. He became a prominent and influential figure in the Chester area and in the wider Diocese as a preacher and public speaker, recognised for his work among the poor, and he was a founder of the Chester Archaeological Society. A leading evangelical (Wilberforce was another friend), he was prominent in the Church Missionary Society. His best known published work is *Remarks on Clerical Education* (1831). He was clearly Bishop Sumner's 'right-hand man' in the Chester years and has generally been regarded as the prime agent in the practicalities of setting up the College. He is still commemorated by annual prizes which bear his name.

James Slade (1783–1860)

Slade was educated at Emmanuel College, Cambridge where, on his graduation as Ninth Wrangler in 1804, he became Fellow and Tutor. He was appointed Canon of Chester and Examining Chaplain by his father-in-law, Bishop Law of Chester, in 1816 and became Vicar of Bolton in 1817. For the next 40 years, he was seldom absent from this manufacturing town except for his terms of residence in Chester. He was in all respects the model reforming clergyman and gained a wide reputation as an inspired preacher. During his time, 14 additional churches were built in Bolton. Slade, like Sumner, believed fervently that the education of the working classes was the key to their mental, spiritual and social improvement. His Sunday Schools became famous, and they were regularly attended by 1,300 scholars aged between six and 40, taught by no less than 100 teachers. In 1846, he founded the Church of England Educational Institution, for boys, girls and evening students. He was also the founder of the Poor Protection Society, the Bolton Savings Bank (1818) and was the first President of the Bolton Missionary Society, founded in 1824.

Horatio ('Horace') Powys (1805–1877)

Powys was born, as his Christian name suggests, in the year of the Battle of Trafalgar, the third son of Baron Lilford. Educated at Harrow and at St John's College, Cambridge, he became Rector of Warrington in 1831. The necessity for improved education was one of his firmest convictions and the strong tradition of church schools in Lancashire owes much to his efforts. He was the first Secretary of the Diocesan Board of Education and was tireless in his efforts to provide schools and to set up an efficient and comprehensive educational system across the Diocese. The crowning glory of his work was the foundation of the two institutions for the training of teachers, Chester College for men and later the institution at Warrington for women. More illustrious and better remembered though some of his fellow Founders may be, it should not be forgotten that Horace Powys was the planner and organiser of the whole Diocesan scheme. He was made Bishop of Sodor and Man in 1854.

Edward George Geoffrey Smith Stanley, 14th Earl of Derby (1799–1869)

Born into one of the grandest and most ancient families of the North West, Edward Stanley was educated at Eton and at Christ Church, Oxford. His aristocratic upbringing was balanced by the strong Anglican evangelicalism of his mother, the daughter of Geoffrey Hornby, Rector of Winwick. He maintained a steady, lifelong sense of duty to the North West. His interests were intellectual as well as those expected of his patrician station, and in 1819 he won the prestigious Oxford Chancellor's prize for Latin composition. Throughout his life, he translated classical authors, as well as contemporary French and German poetry. In 1852, he succeeded the Duke of Wellington as Chancellor of the University of Oxford. In his obituary, published on 25 October 1869, *The Times* characterised him as 'the only brilliant eldest son produced by the British peerage for a hundred years'.

His political career is not our concern here; suffice it to say that he was the first British statesman to become Prime Minister three times and, to this day, remains the longest serving party leader in modern British politics. He was generally admitted to be one of the most effective parliamentary speakers of his time. His underlying philosophy is neatly summarised in a speech he made in the House of Lords in March 1858, in which he said that the age was one of constant moral, social and political progress, in which old institutions should, by judicious changes, be adapted to the increased demands of society. Already to his credit was his forceful advocacy of the great Reform Bill of 1832 (also supported by Sumner) and his drawing up of the Abolition of Slavery Bill, which became law in 1833. His contribution of £10,000 to the relief fund during the Lancashire cotton famine of the 1860s was said to be the largest single subscription to any public fund by an Englishman at that time. As early as 1828, he had published his *Conversations on the Parables for the Use of Children*, in which he explained the parables as moral lessons on the Christian duties of personal faith, charity and humility. Such was the background from which the lustre and influence of his name was added to the Founders' efforts; but he also had some experience of the education of the masses, having introduced grants for teaching under his Irish Education Act of 1831, with a hope that such a system might be introduced in England. It was Stanley who, on 25 January 1839, moved the motion to set up the College.

William Ewart Gladstone (1809–1898)

What further may usefully be said of Gladstone? He is the only man to be four times British Prime Minister and was described by his biographer Lord Jenkins as 'the most remarkable human being who ever held that office'. He was the towering figure of Victorian England. He may be said to have 'opened' the College buildings in 1842 and was the first to endow an annual bursary. Like Stanley, he was educated at Eton and at Christ Church, Oxford. Appropriately, his first speech is said to be the one he made at 'Pop', the Eton Society, in 1825, on the proposition that education was 'on the whole' good for the poor. At Oxford, he was President of the Union and, in 1831, took a celebrated double first.

Unquestionably, Gladstone saw the Church in its traditional role as responsible for the schooling of the people, but was also aware of the desirability of professionally trained teachers. In a significant memorandum of 1838, written for the Committee of Enquiry set up to revivify the National Society, he expressed a hope that schoolmasters might no longer be failures from other professions or 'the wrecks here and there of human energy and hope in other walks of life', but that 'we shall see the position of a schoolmaster made an object of honourable desire, and sought through early training and deliberate purpose by the best and most promising minds'. Admission to training should be by merit and aptitude (tested by examination) and recruitment should not be difficult because 'promising children will relish the idea of promotion to a better status'. This theme was one to which he returned in his speech at the opening of the new College building on 1 September 1842:

> The education of that useful and meritorious class of students, the teachers, would ensure incalculable advantages to the people of these realms and he trusted the day was not distant when they would be spread through the country and be found imparting to others the knowledge they had acquired under the judicious system adopted in Chester.

The Reverend Arthur Rigg, First Principal of Chester College (1839–1869)

By any measure, Rigg was an inspired choice as first Principal on the part of the Committee. He was born in Carlisle on 10 March 1812. His father died when he was only eight. His mathematical and mechanical tastes were evident very early in his private education at Christleton, near Chester, and on the Isle of Man. He entered Christ's College, Cambridge, and graduated as 27th Wrangler in 1835. He was immediately ordained and appointed Senior Mathematical and Philosophical Master at the Royal Institution in Liverpool. In 1837, he married the daughter of James Kendrick, MD, of Warrington, himself the founder of scientific and medical institutions in that town and a subscriber to Chester College. Rigg was appointed Principal of Chester College on 19 September 1839, having been chosen from a large number of candidates. For the next 30 years, he appears to have devoted himself to the College and its attached schools, though he was also active in the Chester Archaeological Society and in the foundation of the Chester Art School. Yet it was the mechanical and natural sciences which pervaded his whole life, most evidently in his book *A Harmony of the Bible with Experimental Science*, published in 1869. He shared the Founders' vision of progress depending on properly trained teachers working in local, often humble, schools; this is neatly illustrated by his use of Wordsworth's lines from *The Excursion* (Book IX) as a question in the admission examination:

> Change wide, and deep, and silently performed,
> This Land shall witness;...
> Expect these mighty issues: from the pains
> And faithful care of unambitious schools
> Instructing simple childhood's ready ear:
> Thence look for these magnificent results!

It was Rigg's efforts which brought the College into physical existence within five months of his appointment. When he took up his post there were no premises, no equipment, no students and no secure finance. The latter deficiency was later addressed through his enterprise in combining the College with a private boarding school and the celebrated 'Science School', which proved so profitable that it was able to subsidise not only Chester College, but the sister institution at Warrington as well.

The Science School was ahead of its time and nationally recognised as one of the most advanced institutions of applied technology in England. Its activities were conducted for the benefit of the whole College; real articles and equipment were made for the use of the teachers and the model practising school and were sold to other educational establishments.

The Foundation

The speed of the Victorian achievement from proposal to reality is astonishing to modern eyes. The formation of a Diocesan Board of Education had only been mooted at a preliminary meeting in the Chapter House of Chester Cathedral on 8 January 1839; a second meeting held at Warrington on 25 January 1839 in the National School House, 'the Great Diocesan Meeting', was to prove momentous. Bishop Sumner opened the proceedings, and he was followed by Horace Powys, who said that the foundation of a Church of England training institution was the most important matter of the day. His speech also contained the germ of the idea for the Science School: 'Parents are no longer satisfied that their children should be instructed in books alone, but that their reading should receive a practical application or be illustrated by experiment'. It fell to Lord Stanley to propose the resolution 'that the Diocesan Board establish at Chester a seminary for the training of masters'. It is recorded that 'the Noble Lord sat down amidst enthusiastic and prolonged applause'. He was seconded by Canon Slade and the meeting concluded at a quarter to four, after five hours of debate. It is fitting therefore that Chester College, now the University, takes its foundation from 1839 and recognises 25 January as its Founders' Day.

A third meeting, convened by Bishop Sumner at the Adelphi Hotel, Liverpool, on 8 February 1839, established the membership of the Diocesan Board and appointed the Training College Committee, with powers to nominate a Principal and to draw up rules and regulations.

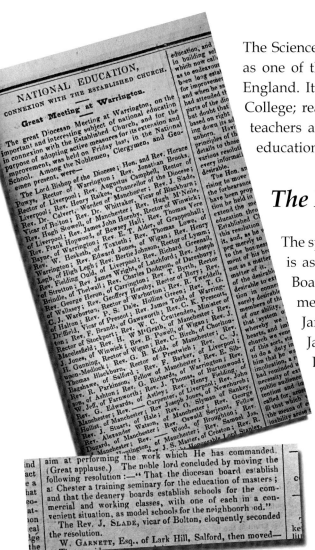

Above: The Warrington National School Building in which 'The Great Meeting' took place

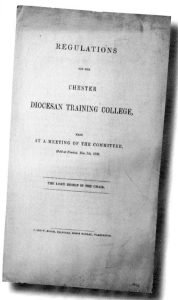

The Buildings

The College opened on 1 February 1840 in temporary premises (now demolished) on the east side of Nicholas Street, with 10 students, a number which increased to 18 by July. The building was described as 'somewhat gloomy' and suffered from bad drainage. On 25 July, Raikes leased additional accommodation for the 'Training Department'. This was the grand mansion in Lower Bridge Street known as Bridge House (subsequently the Oddfellows Hall), Chester's first strictly neo-classical house, built in 1676 for Lady Mary Calverley. Typically, Rigg soon had the students cultivating the large garden at the back of the mansion and installed a lathe, a stone for lithographic printing and a bookbinding appliance in the stable. Nicholas Street was retained for boarding the students. Bridge House was, in fact, briefly considered by the Committee in 1840 for a possible permanent site.

In 1841, the Training School Committee reported 'that the temporary Establishment is now quite full – 26 students being in residence – of whom 6 will be qualified to take situations at Christmas ... and that 11 candidates for admission are already entered on the books'.

Above: The original building, which temporarily housed the College in 1840. The block in which it stood has been demolished and, following road-widening, the site is now part of the southbound carriageway of the inner ring road at Nicholas Street, roughly opposite Grey Friars

Below: The garden front of Bridge House

Below: Bridge House, Lower Bridge Street

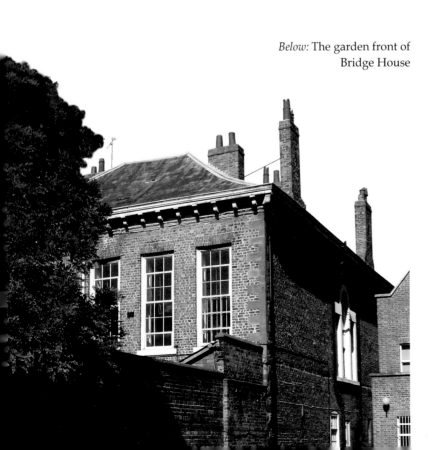

10

'Suitable and creditable' accommodation, as the Diocesan Board put it, was becoming an urgent necessity. Various attempts to find a site near the Cathedral or near St John's Church, and finally between the Liverpool and Parkgate Roads, had failed. An impassioned seven-page letter from Henry Raikes of 23 September 1840 persuaded the Chapter of Chester Cathedral, under its newly installed Dean, the Hon. Frederick Anson, to make a gift of an acre of land in Mollington Lane Field to the west of Parkgate Road, bounded by Chain Lane (later Cheyney Road) to the south, for the site of the new College. The remainder of the field, stretching west towards the canal, was leased, giving a further four acres for recreational purposes.

Above: Dean Frederick Anson

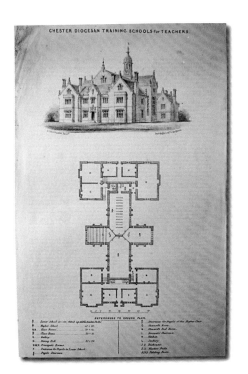

The architects for the new College buildings were John Chessell Buckler and his brother George Buckler. It is not entirely obvious why they were chosen, though the Buckler practice specialised in the Tudor Gothic or Elizabethan style. The prevailing conscious antiquarianism presumably motivated the Building Committee with a sense of what was fitting for an academic institution in an ancient city. Certainly, the Reverend C. Dodgson (father of Lewis Carroll) countered a criticism of cost by saying that it must be a building of taste for a city like Chester. It is possible that Gladstone may have been familiar with the Buckler family's work at Hawarden and nearby Halkyn Castle, though it may be more significant that J.C. Buckler had published *Sixty Views of Endowed Grammar Schools* in 1827. He had also, in 1836, received considerable cachet by obtaining second prize in the competition for rebuilding the Houses of Parliament, which had specified either a Gothic or Elizabethan design. In any event, it is clear that the Bucklers were in favour with the newly formed Chester Diocesan Board of Education, since their design for a model parochial school appeared as the frontispiece to the Board's printed *Report* of 1841.

The new building was opened on 1 September 1842 'with speeches and some little form', as Gladstone recorded in his diary. Proceedings began at 11.00 am with a service in the Cathedral. Canon Slade preached from the text 'Can the blind lead the blind' (Luke 6:39), a sermon which was subsequently printed at Gladstone's request. The company then made their way to the 'great hall or lecture room' of the new building where, with the students lined up near the organ, the 100th Psalm was sung. The Building Committee, represented by Sir Stephen Glynne (Gladstone's father-in-law), Horace Powys and Chancellor Raikes, and the architects then advanced into the centre of the room, led by Raikes bearing the College key, which he solemnly presented to Canon Slade and the General Committee. Mr Gladstone made a speech of congratulation to the Building Committee for their achievement, 'a building intended for the best and noblest purposes, the culture and improvement of the human mind'. The visitors then 'perambulated the apartments: after which they partook of a cold collation, and on the national anthem being sung, the parties retired, highly gratified with the entire proceedings'.

The new building was the first to be erected in the country for the specific purpose of training schoolmasters and, as the minutes of the Committee of the Privy Council on Education stated in 1844:

> It yields to no other similar institution in interest or importance. Neither does it yield to any other in the advantages of its situation, the imposing character and the magnitude of its structure, and the scale of its operations. It is the only building which has yet been erected expressly for the purpose of a training college ... it may serve as a model for every other.

Right: This view clearly shows the rural situation of the College in the early years

The College was welcomed by the city in its early days and pride was expressed by local commentators, who clearly saw it as something of a feather in Chester's cap, and indeed a tourist attraction. The Chester printer and publisher Edward Parry, in his *Panorama of the City of Chester – A Pocket Directory to the Inquisitive Traveller and Curious Tourist* (1843), used a view of the new building as the frontispiece and included a four-page description of the College and its facilities and curriculum.

Gresty's Chester Guide of the 1870s also directed attention to the College as a principal prospect from the Walls and recommended that visitors continue their walk up Northgate Street 'for the purpose of visiting the Training College'.

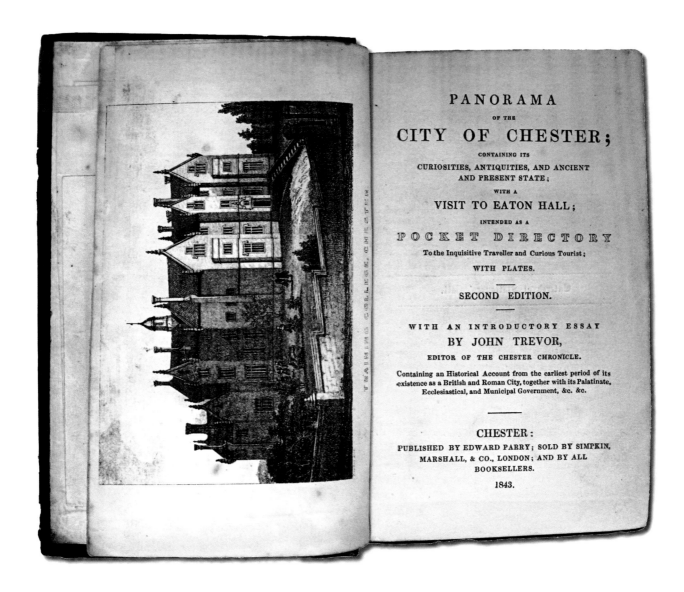

PANORAMA

OF THE

CITY OF CHESTER;

CONTAINING ITS

CURIOSITIES, ANTIQUITIES, AND ANCIENT AND PRESENT STATE;

WITH A

VISIT TO EATON HALL;

INTENDED AS A

POCKET DIRECTORY

To the Inquisitive Traveller and Curious Tourist;

WITH PLATES.

SECOND EDITION.

WITH AN INTRODUCTORY ESSAY

BY JOHN TREVOR,

EDITOR OF THE CHESTER CHRONICLE.

Containing an Historical Account from the earliest period of its existence as a British and Roman City, together with its Palatinate, Ecclesiastical, and Municipal Government, &c. &c.

CHESTER:

PUBLISHED BY EDWARD PARRY; SOLD BY SIMPKIN, MARSHALL, & CO., LONDON; AND BY ALL BOOKSELLERS.

1843.

The Science School was not merely the project closest to Rigg's heart, but was an innovative venture which proved a major contribution to the College's national reputation in its early days. Sir William Crookes, OM, FRS (1832–1919), who was to become President of the Royal Society (1913–1915) and was appointed tutor in Chemistry at the College in 1855, recalled that 'outside London University, there was at that time no better laboratory than that at Chester'.

Though not strictly part of the Training College, it was nevertheless consistent with the intention of the Founders (expressed in Lord Stanley's Foundation Speech) to have a school for middle-class children whose parents wished for a better education for them, but could not afford a public school. It was intended to provide a different kind of education from the old-fashioned Classical curriculum. In fact, under Rigg it took a definite change of direction and the original name, 'The Commercial and Agricultural School' of 1842 had, by the 1850s, become 'The Science College'. Rigg conspicuously stood for progress and the modern world, for science and technology and for the spirit of the Great Exhibition of 1851, to which he organised a special trip for the students. Rigg's son recalled that Sumner, by then Archbishop of Canterbury, accommodated the party from his pet institution at Lambeth Palace.

Right: Sir William Crookes as depicted in *Vanity Fair* by Spy (Leslie Ward), 1900
William Crookes is one of the most illustrious names associated with the College. He was eminent in the fields of chemistry, physics and photography, discoverer of the element Thalium, isolator of Uranium, inventor of the vacuum tube (the Crookes Tube) which made possible the discovery of X-Rays, inventor of anti-polarising glass and the radiometer and he pioneered the use of carbolic acid as a germicide. He was knighted in 1897 and awarded the Order of Merit in 1910

The delightful lithograph below by R.K. Thomas, published around 1847, shows, on the right, the new model National School for 100 poor scholars, where students practised their teaching skills. This replaced the original accommodation in the basement of the main building in January 1843. The principal purpose of the lithograph, however, was to publicise the new Chapel.

The Life of Chester's First Students (as reported by Inspector Moseley in 1844)

Students rose on weekdays at 5.00 a.m. in the summer and 6.45 a.m. in the winter with 'studies' occupying six and a half hours a day, prayers at 7.00 a.m. and 8.30 p.m., three meals, about three and a half hours at intervals for 'industrial occupations', private reading and exercise; bed at 9.00 p.m. Sundays were largely given over to organised worship and Sunday School.

The College Chapel is a building of considerable interest and merit in its own right and that interest is increased significantly given the circumstances of its construction. The original intention was that students should attend services at the Cathedral, but the need was quickly seen for a proper College Chapel where the whole College could assemble. Rigg obviously regarded the project as valuable in furthering his ambitions for the technological content of his curriculum, and the building and furnishing of a new chapel opened up a whole range of possibilities. The students took a hand in raising the necessary funds and lithographed the first 'Appeal' in 1844. They covenanted to dig out the foundations, carve the stone window surrounds and make the fittings and woodwork 'in the hours of recreation', if subscribers would pay for the walls, roof and floor.

The best account of the students' labours comes first-hand from the Reverend Professor Henry Moseley, HMI. In his report of 1844, he paid tribute to the technical work that was going on and noted that each student pursued an industrial occupation: carpentry; cabinet-making; brass-working; bookbinding; painting; turning in wood and metal; stone-cutting; lithography; practical chemistry; gardening; and (somewhat alarmingly) navvying. Moseley writes of the students:

> When I visited the College in November, I found them busily employed in quarrying the stone of which an abundant supply is found on the premises, they had made some progress with the oak carvings, and the stonework of a very beautiful window was nearly completed. Nothing could be more lively or interesting than the scene presented by the grounds and workshops during the intervals of study. In one place the foundations of the structure were being dug out; in another the stone was quarried. In the workshops I found carpenters, turners, carvers in oak and blacksmiths, plying their several trades; and, in a shed, a group of stone-cutters carving with great success the arch mouldings, mullions, and lights of a decorated window.

Beyond doubt then, the decorative stonework and the whole of the interior woodwork, the organ case (designed by Vice-Principal Hutchinson, himself the son of an architect) and the seating was the work of the students themselves, as was some of the stained glass. Donations included £20 from the Dowager Queen Adelaide, £10 each from Mr and Mrs Gladstone, the gift of encaustic floor tiles by Mr Herbert Minton and £500 from Diocesan Board funds. The designer of the Chapel was the influential Manchester architect John Edgar Gregan (1813–55), who gave his services free of charge. Bishop Sumner approved the Order for Daily Services and issued his licence for worship on 18 June 1847. At the opening service on 14 July, Principal Rigg preached from Haggai 2:15: 'And now, I pray you, consider from this day and upward, from before a stone was laid upon a stone in the temple of the Lord'. No doubt the toiling students considered it very well!

Above: Example of the encaustic floor tiles given to the Chapel by Herbert Minton in 1846

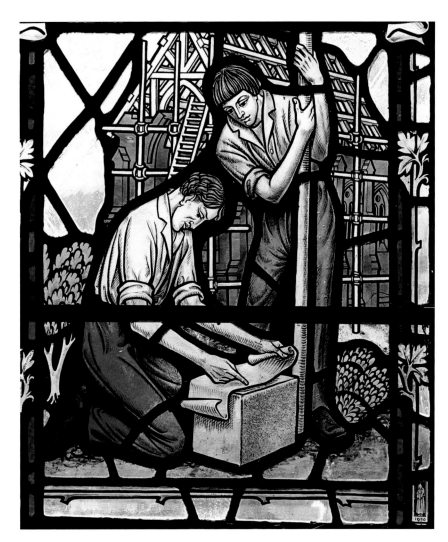

Right: Students working on the Chapel: a panel from the Driver Memorial Window presented to the Chapel in 1950

Sadly, Rigg became, perhaps, a victim of his own success and enthusiasms. As Professor White points out, the College was effectively three institutions in one: the training college for future schoolmasters, an elementary model school where they could practise, and a fee-paying boarding school (the 'Commercial and Agricultural School' later the 'Science College'). Inevitably this led to some confusion in its mission and purpose and compromised Rigg's focus of attention. It remains a great mystery in the history of the college why or how the Governors could have allowed this near fatal situation to have developed. By the time Rigg resigned in 1869, the Science School was thriving, but evidently at the expense of the Training College, which had been the primary object of the Foundation. In fact, student teacher numbers had dwindled from 70 to 11, with no new students entered for the coming year. So bad was the situation that the Diocesan Board passed a resolution to close the Training College from the following Christmas, and advertised in Oxford, Cambridge and in the London *Guardian* for a Principal to carry on the Science School only.

The Reverend Dr J.M. Chritchley (1869–1886)

Dr Chritchley was therefore appointed Principal during the first real crisis faced by the College. He had held the Vice-Principalship for five years. Born in Congleton, Cheshire, he was a graduate of Trinity College, Dublin, and was to prove a second inspired choice. The terms of his appointment on 24 May 1869, 'on the understanding that the Training Department of the College is to be continued, as well as the Scientific School', were somewhat ambiguous in light of the former resolution. He immediately began a long, hard rescue operation. He persuaded the Diocesan Board that resuscitating the Training College was perfectly feasible. As he later wrote, 'I was allowed to try my hand upon its resurrection' and he at once proved his case by recruiting 21 students for admission in January 1870. He solicited support from all available quarters: 60 former students were invited to a social gathering at the College in 1869 and the First Duke of Westminster was persuaded to become a member of the Governing Body. The Science School was gradually phased out and the accommodation taken over by the Training College. At a public meeting in the Town Hall on 27 September 1870, Bishop Jacobson was able to commend the 'excellent quality' of the students going out from the College which, 'if it sustained a brief and transient eclipse, yet we may congratulate ourselves that it has been permitted to sustain itself, and that it is now flourishing and full of promise'.

Any ambiguity in the College's purpose was finally resolved with the closure of the 'Science College' in 1883. Chritchley's achievement cannot be overestimated. Professor White has gone so far as to say that his tenure amounted to a re-foundation of the College, 'He therefore deserves as much recognition as any of the luminaries still remembered as the institution's founders today.'

Above: Chritchley around 1885

Two further significant circumstances aided Chritchley and the College. Firstly, the 1870 Education Act brought in by Gladstone's Government provided for elementary education for all children, and greatly increased the demand for trained teachers. Secondly, the Ecclesiastical Commissioners began to sell off the land, previously vested in the Dean and Chapter, which surrounded the College and thus gave it the chance of increasing the size of the playing fields and providing sites for future building extension. Though there is little evidence that the regime imposed on students was any less strict (and Chritchley certainly kept a very tight control on the meagre finances imposed by the Governors who continued to refuse increases in fees), his era at least saw the appearance of regular sports, such as cricket and football. Another diversion was the recruitment of the students into the Third Battery of the First Cheshire and Caernarfon Artillery Volunteers, with Chritchley himself as the first captain. Perhaps alarming to modern sensibilities, there was on the staff at this time an ex-army drill sergeant whose subject was 'Discipline'. It is a symptom of late Victorian attitudes that military drill became part of the curriculum and Chritchley could speak with perfect confidence of the great importance of the moral effect of military discipline and gunnery training. Perhaps military excursions provided a welcome outlet for students who spent seven hours a day in lectures, with a winter timetable which otherwise gave little time for outdoor exercise.

Below: Playing cricket in front of the College

Above: Cricketers at the College

Below: The College battery won the Queen's prize at Shoeburyness in 1891 and returned to a public welcome

The Reverend A.J. Campbell Allen (1886–1890)

Dr Chritchley was succeeded by the Reverend Andrew James Campbell Allen who was selected from 56 applications largely on the decision of Bishop Stubbs of Chester, the great medieval historian. He was a man of some private means, the Campbell Allens being prominent and prosperous in railways and banking in Ulster. His father had a significant interest in education and had served as secretary of the Joint Board of Managers of the Royal Belfast Academical Institution from 1838 to 1878. He was also the first Registrar of Queen's College, Belfast, and Treasurer of the Belfast Government School of Design. Allen himself was educated at St Peter's College, Cambridge (Peterhouse) and graduated with the glittering prize of Senior Wrangler in 1879. He remained a Fellow of Peterhouse throughout his time at Chester. He has not fared well at the hands of the earlier College historians, principally because he conspicuously failed to 'get on' with the Governors. Yet he wrote a most incisive report on the state of the College on appointment and it is difficult to find fault with what he sought to achieve: improving the standard of entry; removal of some of the harsher restrictions on students (not being allowed to go home in the Easter break, for example); more baths (there was only one with hot water for the whole College!); more drawers and looking glasses in the dormitory cubicles; better laboratory equipment; a new cricket square; a swimming bath; a larger room for examinations; a decent laundry; and a gymnasium, all of which he deemed 'necessary if the

Above: The original College coat of arms which combined the arms of the Diocese of Chester with those of the City

Bottom Right: Staff and students in 1886, with Principal Allen in the middle of the back row

College is to be raised to the position which it should occupy among similar institutions'. As a man who fostered games and was used to Cambridge habits, it is easy to imagine his reaction to Inspector Oakley's objections to students being seen in the streets smoking pipes or lounging in cricketing or boating costumes. It was under Allen that the College magazine, *The Collegian*, was established and it shows the increased freedom, liveliness and bold comment he was trying to foster. We hear of a debating society; rugby was introduced; the College XI played Tranmere Rovers at soccer twice in 1888; and he established the Amalgamated Sports Club in 1890 on the lines of an Oxbridge college.

Allen resigned in 1890, out of some frustration with the national educational system and with the Governors' reluctance to spend money. For example, their havering over a new laboratory ultimately lost the College a valuable member of the teaching staff and threw away a grant-earning subject. He was a loss. He had been passionate in his desire to upgrade the College, improve administration and to introduce a freer and more liberal climate in which students could develop. There were apparently no disciplinary problems in his time, the students found him 'very affable' and the Governors paid him a handsome enough tribute in *The Collegian* on his departure. Professor White designates his tenure as 'An Age of Enlightenment'. He returned to Cambridge and became Vicar of the Peterhouse living of St Mary the Less, and Rural Dean of Cambridge.

Above: The editorial team of
The Collegian, 1888

Below: College rowers on the Dee in 1889

Below: The Chapel Choir drawn from College students and pupils of the College School. Principal Allen at the back

The Reverend J.D. Best (1890–1910)

Allen's successor was the Reverend John Dugdale Best, of Queens' College, Cambridge. He had previously been Vice-Principal of St Peter's College, Peterborough, and Principal of the Derby Training College for Mistresses. Obviously a more conciliatory and diplomatic character, he persuaded the Governors to approve much of what Allen had been seeking both in physical improvements to the College and in relaxations in the regime imposed on students. There were more festivities, students were able to leave the College grounds during free periods from 1.30 pm to 6.20 pm, 'supper' was introduced and the College began to align itself more with the norms of the wider academic world. Notably, he rebuilt the College School, now the Beswick Building in line with the best practice of the time. He installed six new hot-water baths (there had been one for 109 students!), new showers and a students' recreation room. His 20-year Principalship was one of calm and stability whilst academic standards rose. By 1897 Inspector Bennett reported that in most subjects, Chester students were performing above the national average. He was fortunate to have the assistance of some notable tutors: A. E. Lovell, who was also headmaster of the College School, for teaching method and Theodore Ardern, the music tutor under whose inspired leadership the College orchestra was founded. Best also built a new laboratory

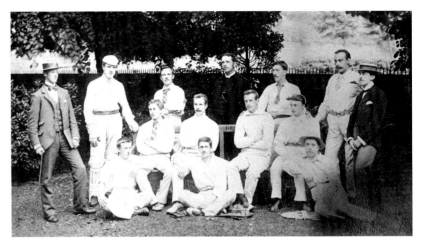

Above: The College 1st XI cricket team, *c.*1896, with Principal Best (back row, centre)

Below left: The Reverend John Dugdale Best and his wife in their motor car at the College

Below: The College orchestra, with Theodore Ardern seated centre, front row

and manual workshop – shades of Rigg – and, in 1896, a typewriter was purchased! Yet, like Allen, he still had to contend with financial stringency. In an amusing aside on the then college motto 'On Chester On' he explained the deliberate misquotation from Scott's *Marmion*: 'Charge, Chester charge! On, Stanley, on!' 'You see', he said, 'Charge, Chester, charge! would be so inappropriate. We don't charge enough. Our fees are the lowest in the land.' Best deserves much personal credit for improvements on all fronts and, with his wife, for the happier atmosphere experienced by students. He is commemorated by a stained glass window in the Chapel. The Collegian reported that 'his amiability has endeared him to all who know him'.

The Reverend Canon R.A. Thomas (1910–1935)

Above: One of the College's first wireless sets built by the students in 1923–1924

Below: Principal Thomas, seated centre, with the teaching staff in 1912. Morrell is standing second from right; Ardern, standing second from left

Best retired in 1910 and the Reverend Canon Richard Albert Thomas, MA, OBE, FSA, was appointed in his place. He was an old boy of the King's School, Chester and was educated at Trinity Hall, Cambridge. He had previously been on the College staff from 1896 to 1905 and was then for five years Vice-Principal of Winchester Training College, before returning to Chester. He had barely got into his stride when the First World War broke out.

The War had a profound effect on the College. Many students immediately joined the forces and by 1915 the remaining number had fallen from 150 to 58. All activities ceased in August 1916 and the buildings were occupied by the displaced St Lawrence College, Ramsgate. Seventy-eight College men died in the war and Principal Thomas served as an army chaplain with some distinction, becoming Acting Chaplain General to the Fifth Army, which bore the brunt of the murderous German offensive of March 1918. For this work, he received an OBE on his return to reopen the College in March 1919. Student numbers rapidly rose to 160 in 1924 and 183 in 1929. The Library was refitted as a memorial to those who had lost their lives and was opened at the Reunion of 21 April 1924. In 1921 the College was affiliated to the University of Liverpool and some members of staff were granted recognition as University Lecturers. Further adjacent land was acquired, bringing the total area up to 22 acres, which was to put the College in a very good position for later expansion.

Like his predecessors, Thomas found much to improve. In 1921 he reported trenchantly to the Governors that 'the buildings at Chester ... bear tragic evidence of the wisdom of making changes or additions without reference to a comprehensive or well-thought out plan'. For example, students still slept in the unheated, open-topped dormitory cubicles of the 1840s. Sadly he did not live to see his ambition for a hostel of study bedrooms built at Chester, though he did have successes despite the war and austerity: the completion of electric lighting throughout the College in 1911, a billiard room in 1924, a sports pavilion and hard tennis courts in 1928–1929 and a new two-storey Arts, Crafts and Science block (now the Thomas Building) in 1931. He inaugurated the College Dramatic Society and the Students' Rag was an innovation in his time.

Above: The Victorian dormitory cubicles

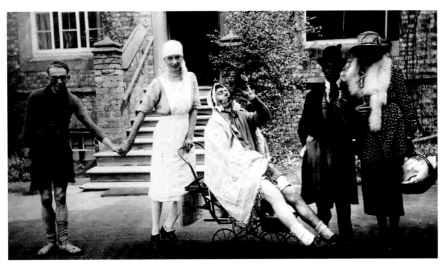

Above: The Rag of 1925 — not an early emanation of the Faculty of Health and Social Care!

In the summer of 1929, the Board of Education placed new demands on the College as a result of the proposal to raise the school leaving age to 15 from 1931. The College responded by taking 185 students in 1929 and 220 in 1930, and proceeded with the building of a new block of lecture rooms. But, with the fall of the Labour Government, the leaving age was not raised and the country entered the great industrial depression of the 1930s. A cut of 10% in teachers' salaries depressed prospects even further. The College faced its greatest crisis to date when, on the evening of 25 November 1932, the Principal received a telegram from the Board of Supervision with the stark message: 'Your College proposed one of three for suspension'. By a process of logic which can only seem to us bizarre, the Board had decided that, in the face of Government cutbacks, the three financially strongest colleges (Chester being one of them, and the oldest) could best afford to close with the hope of possible future reopening, to help the others.

Above: College in the 1920s. The Common Room with its wicker chairs looks slightly less austere than the dining hall and lecture room

24

At this point, the long tradition of the College and the affection in which it was held came into its own. The influence and enthusiasm of the Club of Old Students (over 2,000 strong) was harnessed; letters were written to the Press; petitions were organised and MPs, clergymen, local education departments and teachers' associations in the North West were mobilised. The Dean of Chester, Frank Bennett now threw his weight behind the campaign and drafted the motion to the Church Assembly to save the College with great skill. Illness prevented his personal attendance at the Assembly and so it was that the new Bishop of Chester, Geoffrey Fisher, delivered his decisive speech in support of Dean Bennett's motion in the Church Assembly of 9 February 1933 which saved the day, despite his initial reluctance to rock the Board's boat.

On the morning of the debate, Principal Thomas had wittily informed Fisher that the Assembly's first lesson for the day contained the sentence from Jeremiah 17:11: 'As the partridge sitteth on eggs and hatcheth them not'. (Canon Frank Partridge was the Secretary to the Board of Supervision who had sent the doom-laden telegram.) The text proved prophetic and the closure decision was suspended. The Bishop's speech was to enhance his reputation in his new Diocese of Chester enormously, though, as Professor White has pointed out, Dean Bennett was properly the 'hero' of this close-run battle.

Above: Dean Frank Bennett

The Reverend Canon H.S. Astbury (1935–1953)

Canon Thomas retired in 1935 and was succeeded by the Reverend Canon H. Stanley Astbury, MC, MA, a graduate of Christ's College, Cambridge and previously Chaplain and Assistant Master at Charterhouse. Astbury, like Thomas, had been a chaplain in the First World War, in which he won his MC, and his Principalship was similarly to be interrupted by war, almost directly after the College had completed its 100th anniversary celebrations. Following the Centenary Service in the Chapel on 25 January 1939, Bishop Fisher laid the corner-stone for the new gymnasium. The new lecture rooms were opened on 3 June and the Earl of Derby laid the foundation stone of a new residential block (Fisher House). With war imminent, the Principal noted wryly that a guest had been overheard

to say that the stone was likely to be called 'Astbury's Folly'. War was declared on 3 September and all building operations, except the gymnasium and craft block, ceased. The assembled materials were to be stacked around the site for the next 13 years. With more and more students going into the forces, the College closed in September 1942 and the Vice-Principal took the remaining students to St Paul's College, Cheltenham.

Below: The College in 1939, shortly before it closed down on the Chester site for the duration of the Second World War. Principal Astbury is seated centre with Vice-Principal Morrell on his right, who was to take the remnant of students to St Paul's College, Cheltenham

Below: The distinctive figure of the 17th Earl of Derby laying the foundation stone of the South Hostel (Fisher House) on 3 June 1939. His grandfather, the 14th Earl, had proposed the foundation of the College 100 years earlier. Bishop Geoffrey Fisher is on his right

In June 1940, at the request of the War Office, Principal Astbury took on the role of Commandant of the School which trained over a thousand new Army Chaplains before it moved from Chester in October 1942. At that point, the whole of the College buildings were requisitioned by the War Department as a hostel for the Auxiliary Territorial Service (ATS). On the cessation of hostilities, Astbury was released from the army early in 1945 and in September secured the release of the College premises. The College reopened with both a regular intake and also students under the Emergency Scheme, whose careers had been interrupted by war service. To his credit Astbury endeavoured to liberalise the strict and increasingly irksome student regime which could not survive the generation which had experienced the war. He ended the system of 'prefects', 'monitors', or 'orderlies' which had persisted since Rigg's days as a move towards 'increased liberty and self-government within the College – our students are like other people – the more they are trusted the better they respond'. He must have been deeply disappointed when in 1950 HMI described the College as 'reactionary and old-fashioned in its measures' despite his efforts in difficult times.

The post-war period was to prove the end of the era of old style men's colleges, a change symbolised at Chester by the retirement in 1951 of its celebrated method master, Herbert Morrell. He had joined the College in 1911 and had been Vice-Principal since 1924. When Astbury retired in 1953 it was clear that his successor needed to be a reformer.

The Reverend A.J. Price (1953–1965)

The Reverend Aubrey Joseph Price became Principal in May 1953, the year in which Fisher, by then Archbishop of Canterbury, crowned Queen Elizabeth II. A graduate of Jesus College, Oxford, Price had been headmaster of both St Peter's, York and Wellington, and Principal of Wymondham Emergency College and of Goldsmiths' College, London. The rising post-war birth rate created an unprecedented demand for teachers and some significant developments took place during his

Above: Principal Astbury sits flanked by John L.Bradbury, historian of the College, shortly to become Vice-Principal (left), and Herbert Morrell on the eve of his retirement in 1951 (right)

Memories of student David Lewis (1946-1948)

My first memory of College was of climbing up a cold, stone, spiral staircase which led to the dormitories: Top John, Bottom John, Rookery and Arcadia as they were called – romantic sounding names for sleeping quarters which were anything but that! Each 'dorm' housed about 40 students in tiny wooden cubicles with a sliding door, each room equipped with a bed, a chest of drawers and a corner shelf holding an enamel bowl and jug. There was a small window – not facing a brick wall if you were lucky! Washing facilities comprised two hand-basins in the in the corridor, and two baths in the lower dorm. There was no form of central heating, and it was so cold in the winter of 1947, when the River Dee froze, that one student sleeping in the near-arctic conditions of Arcadia, awoke one morning to find his dentures frozen solid in a glass of water!

time at Chester. The opening in 1953-1954 of the new residential blocks, Astbury House and Fisher House, each accommodating around 70 students, truly marked the end of an era when the dormitories in the Old College, with their names redolent of Victorian college life ('Top John', 'Bottom John', 'Paradise', 'Arcadia' and 'Utopia') were finally vacated. Cold, spartan and divided into 8 ft x 6 ft cubicles, these dormitories

Above: Astbury and Fisher Houses

had been serviced by cold water taps and a curious wooden outrigger, with no visible means of support, known popularly as 'the hanging toilets of Babylon'. On the day Astbury House was opened, the senior student of 1953 compared himself somewhat wistfully to Moses, 'who also saw a promised land which he was not destined to enter'. By 1954 the entire student body could be accommodated at the College. Yet Price and his staff were well aware that colleges of Chester's size (about 150 students) would continue to be vulnerable to any fall in student numbers and did not have the critical mass to meet coming needs; they therefore determined on expansion as their primary aim. New buildings would be needed, as well as regime change. As late as 1959, there was much agonised discussion about whether students should be allowed home at weekends. The doctrine of *in loco parentis* died hard, but many of the old restrictions disappeared very soon after Price's arrival; it was no longer necessary to attend Chapel before breakfast and students were given much greater freedom of movement, especially in the evenings. Whereas in 1953 there had been 151 students, in Price's last term the number had risen to 443. Clearly, staff numbers also had to increase. It is almost incredible that in 1955 the number of academic staff was no more than 12; when Price retired in 1965, it was over 50.

Right: The Art Room, Laboratory and Craft Room in 1964. Is there just a hint that, despite the admission of women, old notions as to division of labour still lingered?

It was a triumphant retirement in many ways. On 4 May 1965, Price had been able to conduct Princess Margaret, the College's first royal visitor, around a substantially rebuilt and modernised College. In 1956, a tutor librarian, Stephen Tillyard, was appointed; he quickly co-ordinated the hitherto scattered subject libraries and created the College's first central library and a recognisable library policy. There was also a new assembly hall, a new dining hall accommodating 440 at a sitting, a crafts block (using the old College School, which had now moved to Blacon), a second gymnasium and smaller hostels to take up to 100 women.

Above: Student Eve Peel with HRH the Princess Margaret, the Bishop of Chester Gerald Ellison, Principal Aubrey Price and Jill Price (By permission of Eve Peel)

The admission of women was, with hindsight, the most epoch-making feature of Price's Principalship. In this hitherto fiercely male preserve, there were dire forebodings amongst staff, old students and friends of the College at any suggestion of 'going mixed' and Price himself was reluctant to break with tradition. But the Ministry of Education was encouraging the training of married women as infant school teachers and, in September 1961, Price interviewed and accepted three women (all married) as the first female students of Chester College. A further major step in the acceptance of women students was the conversion (at last!) of the old building's dormitories into study-bedrooms accommodating 30 unmarried women in 1963.

Below: Carole Froude in one of the first female study-bedrooms in 1964

Sir Bernard de Bunsen (1966–1971)

Sir Bernard was educated at Balliol College, Oxford, and appointed from a background in elementary education in Liverpool and Wiltshire and from a distinguished career as an HM Inspector. More immediately, he had been Principal of Makerere College, Uganda, which he had seen through to transformation into the University College of East Africa and then a College of the University of East Africa, de Bunsen himself becoming Vice-Chancellor.

Arriving in Chester, he was aware that all previous principals had been in Holy Orders and that his 'reverend predecessors ..., like the great headmasters of schools' had exercised an almost exclusively personal control of the College.

He was convinced that teachers-to-be needed the wider company and stimulus of contemporaries preparing for other professions and that colleges of education (as teacher training colleges had recently been officially renamed) should develop, preferably as parts of universities, into campuses where young people with different backgrounds and future careers could meet together. He found to his delight that colleagues who had spent the whole of their careers at Chester, 'who had carried the College through thirty, one through even forty years, like dons at Oxford or Cambridge colleges', readily gave impetus and enthusiasm for this 'little revolution'. Further encouragement came from Gerald Ellison, Bishop of Chester and Chairman of the Governors. The Robbins Report on Higher Education opened up a new prospect for the colleges of education by suggesting their expansion into larger institutions, thereby placing them firmly in the higher education sphere. Despite these encouraging signs, Sir Bernard found that the Department of Education and Science was somewhat hidebound by a fear that colleges would acquire too much independence and that it was, in his words, 'dragging its feet'. He was spurred on by a conviction that, above all, teachers needed confidence through becoming recognised professionals; a university connection was essential if the old colleges were to become centres for training for a variety of professions and could undertake some of the universities' overcrowded undergraduate work. However, he saw his first job as releasing the initiative of colleagues by creating a proper constitutional government for the College which would share some of the powers of the Principal and put him in the place of 'Speaker, enabler and encourager'.

Consequently, a new constitution with an Academic Board came into being, together with an Academic Council on which all academic staff were members. He also inaugurated student representation.

He completed an expansion programme, taking the number of students from 550 to a planned target of 900. New buildings included the Tower Block, named after his predecessor, which provided additional lecture and common room space, with laboratories for physical education and languages. It is amusing to record that the escalating costs of this prominent feature of the Campus led to its being facetiously named 'Price Rise', and in the event it did not receive its planned cladding to relieve its 'brutalist' concrete exterior until 2012. A new students' social centre was built between Fisher House and Astbury House and plans approved for a new swimming bath, which finally opened in 1974.

The establishment of the new four-year BEd degree, combining professional and academic work, was a real innovation and laid the foundations for the stronger academic links with the University of Liverpool that Sir Bernard saw as so crucial to the College's development. Whilst not bearing immediate fruit, he also began to explore the possibility of developing degree programmes in Liberal Studies and Social Sciences.

Above: Sir Bernard de Bunsen and the Bishop of Chester, Gerald Ellison, Chairman of the Governors, at the opening of the 'Aubrey Price' Tower Block in 1968

Below: Price Tower interior

Dr M.V.J. Seaborne (1971–1987)

It fell to Malcolm Vivian John Seaborne to take the College into the next crucial phase of its development and to face one of its severest challenges. A graduate of Gonville and Caius College, Cambridge, he had been, for the past eight years, Senior Lecturer in Education at the University of Leicester. He had previously held posts in educational administration in Chester, Doncaster and Nottinghamshire, had taught in the RAF Education Branch, and had been Head of History at Corby Grammar School.

The academic year 1972–1973 saw the number of students rise to 959, the highest point in the College's history, but it was becoming ominously clear that a major reconstruction of the system of teacher training was imminent. The James Committee Report and the following White Paper, *Education: A Framework for Expansion,* appeared likely to fulfil de Bunsen's ambition by recommending that students training for teaching should, wherever possible, be educated alongside students who had other careers in mind. Colleges were urged to adopt a 'polytechnic' rather than a 'monotechnic' approach. Chester, together with most other colleges of education, began to formulate plans for expanding numbers even further.

Such optimistic expansionist aspirations were short-lived. The White Paper was followed perplexingly quickly by *Circular 7/73*, which dealt in discouraging detail with the effects of the declining birth rate on the demand for teachers and forecast a substantial reduction in the number of students needed to train for teaching in the future. Not only were fewer teachers said to be required, but it also became apparent that the hoped-for increase in the number of sixth formers desiring a more general higher education had failed to materialise on anything like the scale forecast. The scene was thus set for one of the most radical reorganisations of colleges of education which the country had seen.

It is the measure of Malcolm Seaborne's success and of his vision and notable negotiating skills that Chester College emerged intact and stronger from a period during which, nationally, the number of voluntary colleges was reduced from 51 to just 18. The 27 Anglican colleges of education were reduced to 13, of which Chester was one of only nine to remain autonomous and free-standing. In Malcolm Seaborne's words, the College 'survived the storm'. He introduced BA and BSc degrees alongside the now three year BEd degree. This was part of a strategy to phase out non-matriculated entry and to develop a college in which all students were reading for degrees. The survival of the College, when so many suffered closure, depended to a large extent on provision of a greater diversity of courses. This strategy was achieved with the help of the University of Liverpool, which agreed to validate courses leading to a BA in Combined Studies in 1975. This became an Honours degree in 1983, as did the Health and Community Studies degree inaugurated in 1980 and the BSc established in 1985. This was the first successful diversification of the College courses outside teacher training since the pioneering days of the first Principal, Arthur Rigg.

Malcolm Seaborne was, in fact, the first Chairman of the Board of College Studies at the University of Liverpool and he headed a campaign at the University to introduce BA and BSc courses taught by College staff, which the University, at first, had been reluctant to allow. The University's final decision in favour of the colleges was largely due to the excellent standards of teaching demonstrated by College staff and it is testimony to his success that Chester became an affiliated College of the University. His introduction of the BA degree in particular has rightly been described 'one of the most outstanding innovations in the history of Chester College' and proved vital to its survival.

In 1986 the success of the College in recruiting and the change in balance between teacher training and other degree courses meant that 559 undergraduates were taking BA or BSc degrees and 349 were taking the BEd. Fifty-eight mature students were taking graduate or post-graduate courses and 266 part-time students were studying for degrees or diplomas.

In addition to its degree work, the College developed in-service opportunities, for example the Diploma for Teachers of Children with Special Needs, and became a centre for adult education extension classes organised by the University of Liverpool. In 1975, the College also became a centre for the Open University.

Below: Staff and students in 1975, when it was still possible to feature most of the College staff and a significant number of its students on a photograph of this scale

With these new developments came new buildings: a new library opened in 1977; a new resources centre in 1983; a new sports pavilion and a much needed 'student village' of self-catering and self-financing flats was set in train in 1987. In the words of Professor White 'when Malcolm Seaborne ended his tenure as Principal, he was rightly proud of having seen the College through 16 years of almost unremitting challenge'.

The Reverend Canon Dr E.V. Binks (1987–1998)

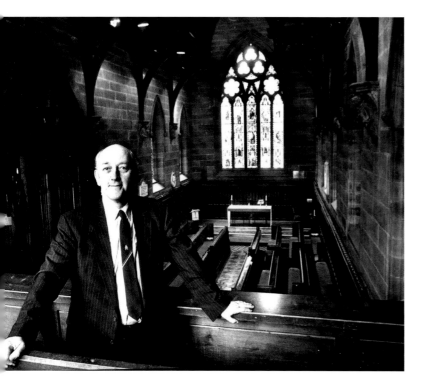

Ned Binks was educated at King's College, London, and had, prior to his appointment, been a lecturer, chaplain and careers advisor at the College of Ripon and York St John and then Head of St Katherine's College, Liverpool. His period at Chester saw expansion on an unprecedented scale. Between 1989 and 1994 alone, the total number of students went up by 224% and the number of part-time students by 419%. Under Binks, the College rode successive waves of expansion as successfully as it had weathered the threats of earlier decades.

The 1988 Education Reform Act changed the system of governance for institutions of higher education, enhancing the powers of principals and giving them considerable freedom of action. Binks, in fact, became the 'Chief Executive' of the corporation. A national policy of increasing student numbers, without a commensurate increase in funding, also offered the former voluntary colleges an opportunity for growth, although only by competing for resources with the rest of the sector. Binks was also convinced that a predominant reliance on teacher education could not alone ensure the survival of the College. In his own words, 'In 1988 we were being given the opportunity to grow and diversify and we had to do both if we were to secure the future of the institution'. His analysis was borne out by Sir Graeme Davies (former Vice-Chancellor of the University of Liverpool, then Chief Executive of the Higher Education Funding Council for England and subsequently Vice-Chancellor of the University of London) at the opening of the new Psychology and Computer Studies Block in October 1995, when he stated publicly that, had Chester and other enterprising colleges not diversified, they would have gone to the wall. The Binks era was to end, once and for all, the still widely held notion that the College was, despite diversification, basically a teacher training college.

However, in 1988, growth and diversification could never have been attempted without the commitment and hard work of the College's academic staff. No greater tribute can be paid to staff during this period than to state that, whilst student numbers rose by 224%, teaching staff

Above: Swimming Club in 1987–1988

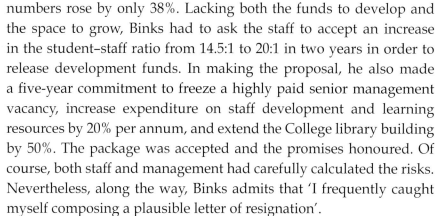

numbers rose by only 38%. Lacking both the funds to develop and the space to grow, Binks had to ask the staff to accept an increase in the student–staff ratio from 14.5:1 to 20:1 in two years in order to release development funds. In making the proposal, he also made a five-year commitment to freeze a highly paid senior management vacancy, increase expenditure on staff development and learning resources by 20% per annum, and extend the College library building by 50%. The package was accepted and the promises honoured. Of course, both staff and management had carefully calculated the risks. Nevertheless, along the way, Binks admits that 'I frequently caught myself composing a plausible letter of resignation'.

Another key factor in the College's expansion was the vigour with which Binks seized the opportunity presented by the Government's 'Project 2000' for the higher education of nurses, which brought them within the scope of the university sector and carried the prospect of an added funding stream from the Department of Health. Acquiring nurse education entailed a competitive process, in which Chester won out over a number of other institutions in the North West. In 1991 the College and the Chester and Wirral College of Nursing and Midwifery combined to provide education and training for 200 students a year, and in 1992 the number increased when student nurses and midwives from Crewe and Macclesfield joined the course, which now led to a Diploma in Higher Education. The Regional Health Authority backed the initiative by financing a new headquarters building on the College site. The extension of the College's influence into the sphere of health

Left: By the mid-1990s, the College's School of Nursing and Midwifery was deeply involved in the development of nurse education in Russia. Professor Dorothy Marriss, Dean of Nursing and Midwifery (third from right), Dr Irina Bublikova, Director of Medical College No 1, St. Petersburg (first from right), with Russian nurse tutors

education and the health services was also exemplified by the Principal serving for five years as a non-executive director of the then Chester Health Authority.

In parallel with growth came increasing academic independence. Accreditation of the College by the University of Liverpool in 1994 lifted the close oversight of academic affairs which had been the condition of affiliated status since the 1920s. In becoming an accredited college, the College acquired greater powers of academic self-determination. On the secure foundations of its Combined Subjects degree, new, more specialised courses were constructed, with curricula which the College itself had devised.

Above: The Reverend Ned Binks, Principal of Chester College, and Brigadier James Percival, OBE, Chairman of the Trustees of the Cheshire Military Museum, signing the memorandum of co-operation between the two institutions on 24 January 1997. This partnership underpinned the MA in Military Studies

Thus, a number of key elements converged: the College rose to the challenge of simultaneous diversification and expansion, and its validating University had sufficient confidence in it to allow it much greater academic independence. These key changes – growth, diversification and enfranchisement by Liverpool – created the preconditions for the later developments of Degree Awarding Powers and university status.

A further significant feature of these years of expansion was the financial premium placed by central Government on the recruitment of part-time students. Binks pursued a policy of encouraging the recruitment of more part-time students and, by 1994, 40% of the College's 4,900 registered students were on part-time Diploma and Master's programmes. However, he also had to ensure that growth in full-time numbers was properly regulated. He proved notably adroit at maintaining a balance between those departments of the College which had the capacity to recruit part-time students and those whose strength lay chiefly in their appeal to full-time undergraduates.

Concern for the employability of students was also a hallmark theme of the Binks era. Having been Careers Advisor at the College of Ripon and York St John, he brought with him to Chester a commitment to strengthening the careers service. He was also a prime mover behind the expansion of Work Based Learning, which secured additional external funding under the highly competitive programme mounted by the Department of Employment in the 1990s to promote enterprise in higher education. It remains a distinctive feature of Chester degrees that students are afforded the opportunity to include a work-based component in their undergraduate studies. It is significant that the employment rate of students following graduation increased consistently and stayed ahead of the national average during Binks's tenure.

Above: Principal Ned Binks, His Grace The Duke of Westminster and Mrs Maggie Taylor, Director of the Enterprise in Higher Education Initiative, at the Initiative's launch in 1990

He pursued two other key policies that he saw as essential for the enhancement of the students' experience: the enlargement of the College's estate, and the raising of the academic profile of the staff.

Below: HRH Princess Margaret opening the Student Village, 1989

Below: HRH Princess Margaret laying the foundation stone of the Molloy Hall, 1989

In addition to new buildings for Nursing and an open-access computer suite, there were added the new lecture hall and performance space, the Molloy Hall, in 1990, the promised library extension in 1991 and a new building for arts and technology in 1992. The old Principal's House of the 1840s was converted into a conference centre in 1988. Also in 1988, St Thomas's Vicarage was purchased and became the home of the English Department, with new student flats being built alongside it in 1992. Very appropriately, the History Department was relocated to Chester's historic Blue Coat School in 1996 where it remained until its move to the Binks Building in 2010.

As student numbers grew and new buildings were added, the profile of the academic staff also underwent significant change. Increasingly, the College recruited staff with backgrounds and qualifications in academic research in order to deliver its newly diversified curriculum. As a direct result of this policy, the College soon acquired the capacity to supervise its own research students; a development underpinned by the decision to introduce generously funded research bursaries for full-time PhD students.

Above: The Vicarage of St Thomas's Church was built in 1880 to the designs of the distinguished Chester architect, John Douglas (1830-1911). It now houses the English Department

Ned Binks took his pastoral role extremely seriously and the welfare of students and staff was not allowed to suffer during this period of growth. He was also acutely aware of his personal responsibility for good stewardship in managing the College's resources. The direction he set for the future was one of steady progress towards university status through growth in student numbers and extension of the range of academic disciplines. Yet, because growth had to be achieved within the national context of a diminishing unit of resource, Binks saw the need to limit indebtedness and to control recurrent expenditure as tightly as Chritchley had done in the 19th century. Thus, by securing financial stability while managing massive expansion, Binks provided his successor with a solid base from which to take the College into the most exciting phase of its history. He bequeathed to his sucessor a favourite aphorism 'always bid for projects that will take the College where it wants to be anyway'.

Below: Chester's historic Blue Coat School, the location of the Department of History and Archaeology from 1996 until 2010

Canon Professor T.J. Wheeler, DL, Last Principal of University College Chester (1998–2005) and First Vice-Chancellor and Principal of the University of Chester (2005 onwards)

Below: The Right Reverend Dr Peter Forster, Lord Bishop of Chester and Chairman of the Governors, now Pro-Chancellor and President of the University Council

The opening years of the 21st century were to prove the most momentous in the College's long history. Professor Timothy J. Wheeler was appointed in succession to Ned Binks at a pivotal point in its development. Educated at the University College of North Wales, Bangor, where he had gained a Doctorate in Psychology, he brought experience of a wide range of institutions, which was to prove invaluable in navigating the course the College was to take. After lectureships in Psychology and Communications at Sheffield Hallam University in the 1970s, Tim Wheeler became Dean of the Faculty of Communication and Human Studies at Dublin City University and, in 1985, Professor and Head of the School of Social Studies at the Robert Gordon University, Aberdeen. Following a period as Senior Visiting Research Scholar at St John's College, Oxford, he became Head of the Department of Communication and Media at Bournemouth University, moving to the Southampton Institute in 1991, becoming Acting Director and Chief Executive in 1997. Much of this work had involved academic and industrial consultancies, in addition to experience in Europe, America and Australia.

To this knowledge of flux and development in institutions of higher education, he brought a personal childhood acquaintance with Chester and had reflected on the 'anomaly', as he put it, of its lack of a university; he saw both the need for such a development and the potential of University College Chester to meet it. He remains puzzled that the city fathers did not seize the opportunity in the 1960s, when the Government invited offers from cities such as Chester for university developments following the Robbins Report.

At the time of his appointment, it is probably true to say that the Governors were looking for a manifesto for change, but had no programme or target date for progression to university status. Indeed, there were still lingering thoughts of becoming part of the University of Liverpool. They were certainly aware that changes in the College's culture, resulting from growth, diversification and the changed character of its staff profile, called for new approaches to its management. The Governors were also seeking to appoint someone who would move the institution purposefully towards university status. Even though his original cautious prediction was that the College would not become a university until 2008 or 2009, Tim Wheeler recalls that, when he first mooted the possibility in the spring of 1998, it was met by some with incredulity. However, Wheeler's ambitions for the College struck a chord with the academic community as a whole and were strongly endorsed by the Chairman of the Governors, Bishop Peter Forster, and by business representatives on the Governing Body.

Above: The opening of the Chester Business School by Sir Howard Davies, Chairman of the Financial Services Authority, in May 2002

Above: Leslie Temple, retired cardiothoracic surgeon and one of the College's most distinguished (and oldest!) Humanities graduates, 2001

Wheeler had a clear view of both the potential obstacles to the College's university aspirations and the strategies which were needed to overcome them. These were, briefly: encouraging and instilling the necessary self-belief in what he perceived as an excellent body of academic colleagues; a continued emphasis on sound finances; sustaining and developing good academic standards throughout the College; and maintaining a strong record in student recruitment. It is significant that, in its last year as a College, numbers for the first time topped the 10,000 mark. With this latter priority in mind, he laid great emphasis on boosting marketing and brought his experience to bear on the whole field of corporate communications. In recent years, the general level of applications had risen by over 300%, from around 6,000 per annum to 25,000. The new University was therefore better placed to 'select', rather than simply 'recruit', students from the outset.

Below: Nursing students

Successful re-tendering for the NHS nursing contract was another pivotal achievement in a highly aggressive and competitive environment. Not only was the existing Chester contract renewed in 1999, but the College received the contract for Halton and Warrington as well. The addition of the School of Nursing and Midwifery represented the

Above: The Binks Building replaced some indifferent earlier accommodation and mobile classrooms and is now a striking and distinguished focal point of the Chester Campus.

Above: HRH, The Princess Royal visiting in 2004 to open the Binks Building

Below: The North West Media Centre on the Warrington Campus, opened by former Education Minister Dr Kim Howells, with Helen Jones, MP for Warrington North

major 'step change' of the early years of the Binks Principalship. The comparable major achievement of Tim Wheeler's early years as Principal was the formation of the Chester Business School in 2000. This development, which Wheeler personally initiated and oversaw, added greatly to the range of vocational courses which the College offered. By 2004, it was possible for the School of Business, Management and Law to take its place alongside the other seven schools (later renamed faculties) of Arts and Media, Humanities, Applied and Health Sciences, Social Science, Lifelong Learning, Health and Social Care (formerly Nursing and Midwifery) and Education.

Simultaneously with these developments, Tim Wheeler pursued a policy of sustained improvement and capital investment in the College's estate. As well as the landmark Binks Building, opened by HRH Princess Anne on 4 November 2004, the College built a new sports hall and a new Health and Social Care block, in addition to extensive upgrading of both teaching facilities and residential accommodation. The years 2000–2005 also saw the unfolding of an ambitious information strategy, with vastly increased investment in information technology.

A significant expansion, however, came with the merger with the Higher Education Faculty of the Warrington Collegiate Institute in 2002. This move was a bold step and not without risks, but the advantages both to the College, which substantially strengthened its position in the North West, and to Warrington, where participation in higher education was comparatively low, were compelling. Warrington Collegiate Institute's Padgate Campus represented a substantial capital asset and a valuable potential revenue stream. The Institute had an especially high reputation for Media Studies and, with the goal of university status in prospect, the amalgamation brought crucial critical mass and enlarged the College's range of subjects and courses. It was a measure of the College's growing significance at both

41

regional and national levels that it was able to secure moral and financial backing for the merger from the Higher Education Funding Council for England and the Northwest Development Agency. As a result of this additional support and a substantial contribution from the College's own resources, a capital building and refurbishment programme was embarked upon which has transformed the facilities and appearance of the old Padgate Campus.

The regional role of the College, which Tim Wheeler had done much to advance, was clear to the Northwest Development Agency and its officers. From their perspective, a university in Chester, especially with the added advantage of the Warrington base, would be a powerful aid to their economic strategy of securing high-value jobs and the people to fill them. In this, they found themselves of one mind with major business supporters such as MBNA, local Members of Parliament, Cheshire County Council, Chester City Council, and Warrington Borough Council.

Size, capacity and regional repute were vital factors in laying the ground for a bid for university status. A final, critical piece in the jigsaw remained – the power for Chester to award its own taught degrees, which was granted by HM Privy Council on 5 August 2003. This key step depended upon a demonstration of the quality of academic provision and the maintenance of standards over a sustained period. Once these powers were gained, the essential pre-requisites for the title of university were satisfied.

Below: Bache Hall, one of the Health and Social Care Education Centres, originally opened by the Rt Hon. John Hutton, MP, with Christine Russell, former MP for Chester

University College to University of Chester

Above: Professor Glyn Turton and Professor Graeme White

In September 2004, after intensive, careful preparation, the University Title Group, led by Professor Glyn Turton, Senior Assistant Principal, and Professor Graeme White, Dean of Academic Quality and Standards, was able to deliver the application for the title of university to the Office of HM Privy Council. Great credit is due to this pair and to the College as a whole for being in a state of preparedness when the then Education Secretary Charles Clarke rather suddenly gave an opening for teaching-led institutions to become universities. The opportunity, once it arose, was grasped vigorously and decisively by the Principal, Governors and the staff and students.

A tantalising period followed. On Monday, 21 March 2005, the College received official confirmation that it had met the criteria for university status. The long wait for confirmation of the title of university by order of HM Privy Council was agonisingly delayed by the General Election of May 2005, but the eagerly awaited document, as momentous in the College's history as the Founding Resolution of 25 January 1839, was issued on 22 July 2005.

University College Chester became the University of Chester officially on 1 August 2005. His Grace the Duke of Westminster agreed to become the University's Foundation Chancellor, with Professor Tim Wheeler as its first Vice-Chancellor. The Assistant Principals were now designated Pro-Vice-Chancellors and Academic Board was renamed the Senate, with the Governing Body taking the title of the University Council and its Chair, the Right Reverend Dr Peter Forster, Lord Bishop of Chester, becoming Pro-Chancellor and President of the University Council.

A week of celebrations in honour of the institution's new status took place in September 2005. Appropriately, these began at Warrington, where 'the Great Diocesan Meeting', which led to the founding of the original College, had taken place on 25 January 1839. One hundred and sixty-six years later, the Mayor of Warrington attended a VIP lunch that marked the inauguration of the Warrington Campus as part of the new University of Chester. The social highlights at Chester included a ball, attended by 1,500 members of staff, their families and friends, and a formal banquet for 300 invited guests, both of which culminated in a spectacular firework display on the sports field.

The climax of the week was the formal inauguration of the University, which took place on 25 September 2005, in Chester Cathedral. The ceremony was attended by civic dignitaries and over 100 members of staff. William Bromley-Davenport, Lord Lieutenant of Cheshire, read HM Privy Council's official proclamation, authorising the establishment of the University, concluding with the declaration: '**Fiat Universitas Cestriensis**'. The Duke of Westminster then formally accepted the office of Chancellor and was installed as the first holder of the position.

Above: Illuminating the night sky over Chester, to herald the University's launch

Left: The official procession leaves the Cathedral at the end of the inauguration ceremony led by the University's new Chancellor, His Grace the Duke of Westminster

Below: Luncheon guests at Warrington celebrating the achievement of University status

The University: Progress and Expansion

The clear priority for the new University in 2005 was to consolidate its reputation for excellence, building on its traditional strengths and continuing to develop those strategies and policies which had served it so successfully in previous years. But it could not rest on its laurels in an increasingly competitive environment. It needed to act decisively when new opportunities arose to strengthen its position. The history, traditions and corporate strength of the institution, combined with its reputation for innovation and for student support, were already leading to healthy competition for places on its degree courses and autumn 2005 saw a record number of 12,600 student admissions. The major concern of the Vice-Chancellor and his senior colleagues was not, however, with numerical growth for its own sake, but with the enhancement of quality and the expansion of activities into more areas of the research, applied consultancy and services to businesses in the region and beyond.

The main strategic objectives for the next few years remained the continuing diversification and development of the programmes being offered: the accelerated development of the Foundation Degree programmes in collaboration with further education establishments in the region, the growth of the research portfolio and obtaining Research Degree Awarding Powers.

It is not possible within a book of this size and purpose to record all the developments which have taken place over the 10 years of the University's existence. Even if it were attempted, it would do scant justice either to them, or the many members of staff to whom credit is due, to give a long and inevitably breathless catalogue of achievements which are chronicled in the series of Annual Reviews now produced by Corporate Communications. The following pages therefore seek to give some flavour of the outstanding developments of an astonishing decade by means of pictures and thumbnail sketches which are examples only of a much wider and deeper picture. They are grouped into six broad themes.

Above: The first Esquire Bedel Ray Williams carrying the University's Mace, a symbol of its new status. It was specially designed and hand-crafted by Mappin & Webb, and first used at the inauguration ceremony. Sponsorship was kindly provided by the MBNA Foundation

Left: Graduates in front of the Eastgate Clock

Expanding the Curriculum

Whilst holding true to the founding principles of the original College, the University has developed both its traditional academic subjects and massively expanded programmes with a vocational element and those which address pressing social needs.

The Undergraduate Prospectus for 2016 lists 106 degree courses embracing single honours and in excess of 700 combined course combinations across eight faculties.

Well-established work based learning placements feature in most undergraduate degrees giving students excellent opportunities to enhance their skills in preparation for employment.

At the time of writing, over 95% of recent graduates are in work or further study six months after graduation – one of the best percentages of any North West university. In fact the Government's annual employability survey has shown Chester consistently outperforming both regional and national averages.

Above: Teacher Training students on school practice

Above: Forensic Biology students on a scene of crime exercise

Above: Media students filming an interview

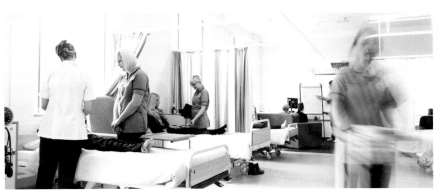

Above: Nursing in the clinical skills lab

Above: History students with Dr Donna Jackson researching John Lennon's childhood garden at Mendips

Above: Fine Art students in their studio

Research

Above: Vice-Chancellor, Professor Tim Wheeler, and Senior Pro-Vice-Chancellor (Research), Professor David Cotterrell, with the letter formally acknowledging RDAP status

Below: Gladstone Fellowship PhD student, Heather Ashcroft who conducted her research in partnership with Alder Hey Children's Hospital

The strategy of fostering research had hardly figured before 1992 though good progress had been made when the application of University status was submitted with the help of Professors Turton and Cotterell. This set out the University's ambitions for research, making a clear and compelling case. The approach was vindicated in October 2007, when Chester became the first of the institutions granted university status in 2005 to be awarded Research Degree Awarding Powers by HM Privy Council. The exceptional speed of this success was a notable achievement and enhanced Chester's reputation as a centre for specialist research expertise. In its first full year, the University received £865,000 in research income and now it is the University's second raison d'être after undergraduate teaching.

Progress was rapid and impressive. HEFCE's Research Assessment Exercise in 2008 classified work in History, English, Sports Sciences and Performing Arts as 'World Leading' and drew attention to the 'International Excellence' of research in Allied Health, Mathematics, Social Work and Social Policy, Geography, Theology and Art. In 2013 Chester was one of 11 universities to gain the HR Excellence Award from the European Commission. The 2014 Research Excellence Framework assessed 16 areas of the University's research, all of which featured internationally excellent work, and 14 featured 'world leading research'.

Chester is also one of comparatively few UK universities to have its own publishing operation, a major enhancement to the profile of research, and to the University's widening reputation. The University of Chester Press aims to disseminate excellent, peer-reviewed original research and other creative work from within the University, together with publications having a relationship to the history and culture of the area. The Press has published more than 50 titles, including the peer-reviewed Issues in the Social Sciences series, the Cheshire Prize for Literature anthologies and a diverse range of academic titles.

By 2015 the University's eight faculties were offering 125 postgraduate programmes covering MA, MPhil, MSc, MBA, MRes, LLM, MEd and MPH. Doctoral Research now includes doctorates in education (EdD), business (DBA) and a range of professional disciplines (DProf) as well as the traditional PhD.

Partners and Outreach

The potential breadth of experience now available to students at the University of Chester is amply demonstrated by a wide range of opportunities offered by 12-month international exchange programmes encompassing 300 destinations in 125 countries. Students can also widen their experience with learning placements in six of the seven continents. In addition, it is a partner in the Santander Universities scheme which provides scholarships, travel awards and research funds for work and research in more than 20 countries, including Brazil, Mexico, Argentina, Portugal and the UK. The University has a thriving Erasmus exchange programme for staff and students which allows study, research and work based learning in a range of European countries, while the International Student Exchange Programme provides opportunities to experience university life worldwide.

Above: Outreach work with schools

Nearer to home, the University has developed its Foundation Degree programmes in collaboration with further education institutions in the region, in such subjects as Adventure Sports Management, Food Chain Management, Health Informatics and Laboratory Technology. Warrington Collegiate was the first of these institutions to gain Associate College status in 2006 and Reaseheath College, West Cheshire College and Isle of Man College have followed suit. The Faculty of Health and Social Care also has partner NHS sites in Chester, across Cheshire and the Wirral.

Above: Santander Universities Director in the UK, Luis Juste, signing the partnership agreement with Vice-Chancellor, Professor Tim Wheeler

The University continues its commitment to widening participation for those groups which are under-represented in higher education. This is evidenced by its outreach work engaging with almost 12,000 students a year, extending from primary school pupils through to mature college students from across the region and beyond. The activities include campus visits and talks in schools and colleges, with the aim of encouraging students to consider their future aspirations while gaining an insight into the opportunities provided through higher education.

Below: Helena Kennedy Foundation 'Sanctuary Foundation Award' student Taudzwa Gunde

Above: Student Hannah Cawley in Tanzania

Above: Rowley's House, University Centre Shrewsbury's historic administration building

Above: Teaching facilities at The Guildhall, Shrewsbury

Below: One of the most important research libraries in Wales, Gladstone's Library in Hawarden, is an Associate Research Library of the Faculty of Humanities and has a strategic partnership with the University

Working in a completely new kind of partnership with Shropshire Council and with a curriculum developed with local businesses and industry, the University has set up the new University Centre Shrewsbury. Under its first Provost, Professor Anna Sutton, it will provide a different type of opportunity for students with some non-traditional academic structures and four main thematic areas of study: medicine and health, sustainable business and community development, societal innovation and design, heritage and the built environment. With an ambition for an eventual student intake of 2,000, the Centre will expand its student accommodation over the next two years. Teaching currently takes place in the riverside location of Shrewsbury's Guildhall.

In 2010 the Department for Education made the University an Accredited Schools Provider for academies and free schools, one of the first organisations in the country to be recognised in this way. The University of Chester Academies Trust (UCAT) is directly responsible for secondary schools in Ellesmere Port (UCEA), Northwich, Warrington and Kidsgrove along with primary schools in Chester (University of Chester Free School, UCFS), Kidsgrove and Weaverham. UCEA moved into its new multi-million pound building in 2012 and UCFS has grown into a very successful school that brings children back into the heart of Chester. UCAT academies are having a growing impact on the learning of thousands of children and young people, as part of the University's continuing commitment to lifelong learning in the local communities it serves. Chester College had, as part of its original buildings, a 'Model School' for 100 pupils that opened in 1843 and so the tradition of running schools may be said to have been revived, and on a much larger scale.

Below: University of Chester Free School

Building for the 21st Century

A few statistics speak for themselves when seeking to give an impression of the scale of improvements over the past decade:

- The Chester Campuses have had around £117million invested in buildings and facilities.
- The Warrington Campus has similarly benefited from a £17million investment.
- The Thornton Science Park, comprising 66 acres and 1,100,000 sq. feet of buildings is valued at over £100million.

The rapid increase in student numbers, together with the rise in the number of programmes of study, have made an extension in teaching accommodation inevitable, a process well underway when university status was achieved.

Above: The Price Tower was vastly improved by a complete overhaul, including smart cladding to the previous rather grim concrete exterior, in 2012. With its heraldic sign it now establishes its dominant presence on the north Chester skyline

Left: The Westminster Building

The Westminster Building, opened officially on 25 May 2007 by His Grace the Duke of Westminster, was the first of the major new building projects to be completed after the obtaining of university status. The high standard of the construction of the building led to its receiving a Cheshire Built in Quality Award. It is environmentally sensitive, with a 'nature roof' incorporating a low maintenance layer of vegetation for effective insulation and drainage and, internally, movement-sensitive lights in offices to save energy.

Below: Vice-Chancellor, Professor Tim Wheeler, and Pro-Chancellor and President of the University Council, the Right Reverend Dr Peter Forster, the Lord Bishop of Chester, with University Chancellor, His Grace the Duke of Westminster, as he officially opened the building named in his honour

Right: Tutor block and courtyard amphitheatre at Kingsway

Above and below: Contemporary Art Space Chester

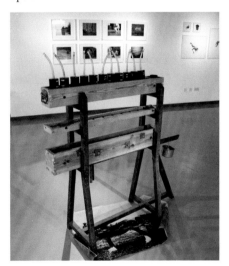

Below: The alumni exhibition by Fine Art students from the last decade at CASC

Another Faculty needing greater accommodation at Chester was the newly designated Faculty of Arts and Media. The University was able to obtain the former Kingsway High School site in 2005 and the first phase of an extensive, multi-million pound re-modelling was completed in September 2007, transforming the Kingsway Buildings into a dedicated base for the Faculty's activities in Chester. Its departments, now much closer together, have increased the potential for interaction between creative disciplines.

Kingsway includes extensive studio space, a 136-seat multi-purpose performance venue with retractable seats, rooms for sculpture, textiles, 3D printmaking and a hot room for castings, two Graphic Design laboratories and studio space, sound and video editing booths, a photographic studio, a reprographics room, communal areas for breakout sessions and an outdoor performance space. The Contemporary Art Space Chester (CASC) was the first dedicated contemporary art space for the city.

Below: Kingsway Buildings

A new £2million Chester Students' Union headquarters, to service the social needs of the increasing numbers of students was built on the Chester Campus and has vastly enhanced facilities for sport and social activities.

The Best Building houses the Departments of Geography and Development Studies and Social Studies and Counselling and the facilities include a map and open access resource room, a Geographical Information Systems (GIS) laboratory and a soils laboratory. Among other uses, this building acts as the focal point for the innovative Carbon Neutral Project, the Natural Hazard Management course and the pioneering Centre for Research and Education in Psychological Trauma.

At Warrington, the process of developing and improving the quality of the Campus's building stock continues, notably with the transformation of the former Derek Newton Theatre into the North West Media Centre. The links with the BBC at MediaCity means that students gain experience in a number of BBC departments, in order to equip them with the necessary skills and expertise to pursue a career in media. The Hot Room on the Campus provides a joint staff and student opportunity to engage with commercial media projects such as the successful advertising campaign which won Warrington host town status for the 2013 Rugby League World Cup.

Above: Chester Students' Union Building

Above: GIS Laboratory in the Best Building

Below: The refurbished Bar and Club Twenty/10 at Warrington

Below: Broadcasting for the Cat student radio station at Warrington

Below: Counter Supervisor, Ann Vickers demonstrates digital technology to HRH The Duke of Kent in the Broomhead Library, watched by Director of Learning and Information Services, Brian Fitzpatrick

Above: The Broomhead Library

The Broomhead Library project was funded entirely by a £2.35million capital grant from the Higher Education Funding Council for England. It was opened officially by HRH The Duke of Kent on 8 February 2008.

The three-storey Tucker Building nearby serves a dual purpose: as a Warrington base for the Faculties of Business, Enterprise and Lifelong Learning and Education and Children's Services, offering excellent teaching facilities; and as a Business Centre, providing a hub of expertise and support services for local and regional companies. The Building is at the forefront of eco-friendly design, meeting stringent Building Research Establishment Environmental Assessment Method (BREEAM) standards with its energy efficient movement sensors for lights and water taps, and minimal mechanical heating and ventilation. More than 80% of the £3million cost of the building was provided by the Northwest Regional Development Agency.

The Warrington Campus has become a focus for the University's work across both the Public Services and the Creative Industries. The former embraces engagement with Early Years and Primary Education, with Youth Work and Sports Coaching, with Nursing and Social Work and, in partnership with Cheshire Constabulary, with Policing and Investigation. Under the Creative Industries umbrella the Campus brings together Business and Events Management, Marketing and Public Relations, Advertising, Radio, Television and Commercial Music Production, Digital Photography and Journalism. Trans-professional working is a key theme for Warrington's work in Public Services, and the Campus's work across the Media addresses employability in a rapidly shifting world of changing and converging media platforms.

Below: The entrance
to the Tucker Building

Right: Police Specials training
launch in 2010

The University's acquisition of County Hall, one of the principal public buildings of Chester, built between 1938 and 1957 for Cheshire County Council was a spectacular addition to teaching facilities and further manifested the University's stamp on the city. The impressive river front building was sensitively remodelled at a cost of £12.5million, providing over 100,000 square feet of office space, teaching accommodation and library facilities with all the latest technology. The former Council Chamber was converted to a 200-seat lecture theatre with retractable seating and a large screen with the latest audio-visual equipment, capable of showing widescreen, Blu-ray and HD films. Opened in autumn 2010 the Riverside Campus, houses the Faculties of Health and Social Care, and Education and Children's Services, together with support departments such as Marketing, Recruitment and Admissions. The conversion features purpose-built clinical skills labs for nursing and midwifery students that recreate a controlled, but realistic, hospital ward-based environment, while art and design studio spaces, technology and science laboratories and an art therapy room replicate school settings. Office facilities are provided for the Senior Management Team and the University's Governing Body.

Above: The former Council Chamber

Above: Students at the Riverside Campus

Below: View of the Riverside Campus across the River Dee

The basement of the building houses the Faculty of Health and Social Care Riverside Museum of curiosities from the world of medicine, nursing, midwifery and social work, together with its exhibition 'The First World War: Returning Home'.

In the words of Dr Malcolm Rhodes, Senior Pro-Vice-Chancellor (Resources), writing in 2010:

> This latest refurbishment has been the largest and most complex ever undertaken within the University and required a series of logistically complex and time critical relocations during the summer of 2010, involving some 450 academic and support staff across nearly 20 departments and locations.

The launch of the University's incubation hub in Chester has meant that entrepreneurs and established businesses from Cheshire and the North West can now access additional business expertise and support. Almost £6million was invested in the Riverside Innovation Centre (RIC), located next to the Riverside Campus, which offers a variety of help to develop untapped business potential. Jointly funded by the European Regional Development Fund (ERDF), the RIC was the first of its kind in Chester and provides city-centre incubation premises for up to 15 new and existing businesses. In addition, the Centre focuses on support for existing businesses seeking to fulfil their economic potential. It features a number of key services and purpose designed

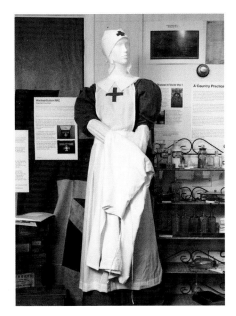

Above: Faculty of Health and Social Care Riverside Museum collection

Below: The Seaborne Library (pictured below) and Allen Building also saw a 25% increase in space for learning resources facilities

facilities including a 200-seater conference suite, break-out rooms, two networking business lounges available on a free drop-in basis, and meeting rooms for hire.

Business support is provided on site with a number of key partners from the business community based at the Centre, including the West Cheshire and North Wales Chamber of Commerce.

Early in 2013 came one of the most significant announcements in the history of the University. Through the generosity of Shell UK, who wished to give something back to the locality, their famous Thornton Research Centre was gifted to the University of Chester for £1, enabling one of the biggest public–private sector collaborations the country has seen. The £240million site has now become the Thornton Science Park and houses the new Faculty of Science and Engineering (the University's eighth faculty and the country's first engineering faculty to launch for two decades). Subjects now offered include Chemical Engineering, Electronic and Electrical Engineering, Physical Sciences, Chemistry and Biotechnology, Computational Engineering and Science and Cyber Security.

Above: Riverside Innovation Centre (RIC)

Below: The Rt Hon Iain Duncan Smith MP with Professor Graham Smith, Head of Natural Sciences, during a visit to Thornton Science Park

The North West Food Research Development Centre (NoWFOOD) is a state of the art research and development facility located on the Parkgate Road Campus, made possible by ERDF and University of Chester funding. Opened in 2014, it provides a centre of excellence for food science and technology for producers across the region and has facilities designed to make a direct contribution to the success of the food industries in Cheshire and the North West.

In 2015 the University acquired a building on the south bank of the Dee as prominent as the former County Hall on the north side. This was the former Western Command Headquarters built for the army in 1937 and flamboyantly extended by a banking corporation in a classical style in the late 1990s. Speaking of its prominent colonnaded portico the Chester volume of the *Buildings of England* series ("Pevsner") describes it as 'looking (from a distance) like a temple from Palmyra between the trees'. With splendid views across the Dee to the city and with two and a half acres of gardens and grounds it now provides a superb setting for the Chester Business School. It has been developed to provide a 250-seat lecture theatre and dedicated library and PC suites. It is now known as the Queen's Park Campus.

Above: Inside the NoWFOOD Centre and the Northwest Human Milk Bank which is based at the Centre

Below: 175th anniversary fireworks   *Below:* Churchill House at the Queen's Park Campus

Student Accomodation

Accommodation for students had been an abiding problem almost from the College's foundation and lack of finance from the Governing Body was the bugbear of succeeding Principals. It had become a positive embarrassment by the 1930s and led to an over-reliance on lodgings which in the crisis of 1932–1933 threatened the College's very existence. This situation persisted well beyond the 1960s. It is therefore refreshing to look at recent improvements in student accommodation into which the University has invested over £22million in recent years.

Above: Grosvenor House   *Below:* Sumner House

The University and the Community

Service to the surrounding population has always been a key element of the University's mission. The ideal of community service can be expressed formally through curriculum opportunities and also through the historic tradition of volunteering. This remains a major component of student and staff engagement with local organisations and charities, and was celebrated in spectacular fashion on 19 July 2007 when HRH The Prince of Wales, accompanied by HRH The Duchess of Cornwall, became the most senior member of the Royal Family so far to visit the Chester Campus. The royal visitors met with students and staff who support a variety of organisations in their free time, as well as representatives of other local community initiatives. In 2012 students and staff contributed 23,250 hours of voluntary work in the area and by 2014–2015 this figure had risen to 32,390 hours.

Above: HRH The Prince of Wales is congratulated on being awarded an Honorary Doctorate by University Chancellor, His Grace the Duke of Westminster on 19 July 2007

Below: The tradition of volunteering

During his visit in July 2007, the Prince of Wales received a Doctorate of Letters, *honoris causa*, thus joining an increasing list of distinguished individuals, including The Duke of Westminster and the then Poet Laureate, Sir Andrew Motion, as an honorary alumnus of the University. This list has continued to grow in the intervening years and includes such prominent figures as Dame Joan Bakewell CBE; The Most Reverend and Right Honourable Dr John Sentamu, Archbishop of York; Terry Waite, CBE; Sir Ian Botham OBE; Loyd Grossman OBE; Tim Firth; Sue Johnston OBE; Phil Redmond OBE; Estelle Morris, The Right Honourable Baroness Morris of Yardley; The 19th Earl of Derby (descendant of the 14th Earl of Derby, one of the Founders of the institution); Sir Tony Robinson; Professor Alan Emery FRSE; Beth Tweddle OBE; The Right Honourable Frank Field MP; Sir Ranulph Fiennes OBE; and the Singh Twins.

The University's commitment to the community was further recognised when Chester Students' Union (CSU) won the Community Relations category at the National Union of Students (NUS) Awards. This event celebrates excellence in the student movement and the contribution which students and students' unions make to the lives of students and the areas in which they live.

Above: Chester Students' Union with the NUS Award

Another example of community involvement is the use of the creative talents of the University's multimedia experts to provide digital media skills for the acclaimed production, *The Creation*, a theatrical collaboration between Chester Mystery Plays and Theatre in the Quarter, which told the Biblical version of how the world began. The Project developed motion graphics, video and stills animations for the stage screen during the performance at the Roman Amphitheatre during Chestival 2011.

Above: Business student James Taylor publicising the Big Green Makeover which inspires students and staff to reduce their carbon footprint on and off campus

Below: The Creation

The Cheshire Prize for Literature was inaugurated in 2003 as The High Sheriff's Cheshire Prize for Literature and is administered by the University. This competition rewards original and previously unpublished work from authors with a Cheshire connection. The High Sheriff's Awards for Enterprise recognise outstanding businesses in Cheshire on an annual basis. It is run by the University and attracts multiple sponsors. All these community initiatives emphasise the increasingly important role played by the University in Cheshire, the North West and beyond.

Above: Dr Pete Waterman at the Awards for Enterprise

Above: Award -winning student film-maker Mercy Liao, BA Religious Studies (2007), behind the lens

Below: The 2014 Cheshire Prize for Literature winners with the High Sheriff Mrs Susan Sellers, Dr Brian Cosgrove (far left, Cosgrove Hall Films), judges and (centre back) John Richards OBE, DL, the founder of the competition

The University celebrated the 175th anniversary of its foundation through a range of events in 2014 and 2015 including the Manchester Camerata's specially written production of *On Chester On* with local school children in Chester Cathedral; The Cathedrals Group's Choirs' Festival; firework displays; two lectures by the Right Reverend and Right Honourable Dr Rowan Williams; anniversary balls for staff and community members; a joint nostalgia event with the Chester Grosvenor Hotel; a special Founders' Day service with an enactment of the founding of the institution; the unveiling of the anniversary quilt created by staff, alumnae and members of the community; a series of watercolour paintings of graduation by former student Thomas Plunkett, President of the Royal Watercolour Society; a celebratory event for the 65th anniversary of the Warrington Campus; charity and sporting events; and a visit by His Royal Highness Prince Edward the Earl of Wessex to the Riverside Campus.

Above: Former Archbishop of Canterbury, The Right Reverend and Right Honourable Dr Rowan Williams, now Master of Magdalene College, Cambridge is Gladstone Professor of Literature and Theology at the University of Chester

Above: The 175 Snowdon Walk

Below: The High Sheriff Mrs Susan Sellers with the Lord Mayor of Chester Cllr Bob Rudd at the unveiling of the anniversary quilt

Above: Visit of HRH the Duke of Wessex to the Riverside Campus

Into the Future

Extending a 'history' into an era of unprecedentedly rapid change is never easy and to speculate on the future can be fraught with danger. Many things will be seen as crucially important in the fullness of time which are not immediately apparent and as the preceding pages amply demonstrate, innovations have consistently been overtaken by even more significant expansion. For example, buried within the latter part of this narrative is the response of the University to the digital revolution and the use of technology in research, teaching and communication and delivery of course materials. In this overwhelmingly digital age it is amusing to recall that as recently as de Bunsen's time the College possessed a single photocopier referred to reverently as 'the Rank Xerox machine'; a second was added in 1975! The University's strategy has conspicuously addressed this challenge. Similarly, it is too early to analyse the effects of shifting government policy, of social engineering both deliberate and accidental, and the vagaries of funding and the global financial climate. More than at any other time, universities are exposed to market forces and have been said to be entering an era of 'survival of the fittest'. What, for example, will be the long-term consequences of the highly political introduction of tuition fees? The University has to date successfully negotiated this upheaval and student numbers have been more affected by Chester's policy of raising admission criteria than by purely financial considerations.

The only indicator is track record and here, the first decade of the University gives overwhelmingly positive indications. Expansion in terms of numbers, facilities and buildings has been chronicled in some detail, but we need also to 'look for results', as Principal Rigg put it back in 1839.

Right: Declan Jarrett, Students' Union President with Jack Mason and Kat Edwards (Vice-Presidents) presenting the Loyal Address and Humble Petition on behalf of the University to Her Majesty the Queen. Photo © George Thornton, Warrington Borough Council

At the time of writing, Chester has one of the highest rankings for graduate employability in the North West. It works with over 1,500 local and regional employers and organisations to provide opportunities for Work Based Learning and has established a highly successful Graduate Head Start (GHS) programme as part of a range of measures to improve employment prospects even further.

Another achievement, which again felicitously recalls the origins of Chester College, is the latest Ofsted rating of the University's teacher training provision as 'outstanding in every category'. It is appropriate to note here that it is, in fact, the Faculty of Education and Children's Services which still embodies the University's origins and carries the heritage of 175 years. Under its Executive Dean, Professor Anna Sutton, it has doubled in size over the past 13 years and now offers, in addition to Initial Teacher Education, continuing professional development to in-service teachers and the wider workforce of schools and services to children, with programmes at undergraduate and doctoral levels. The success in teaching also reaches across other academic departments in the University, resulting in its position as a top quartile Higher Education Provider for student satisfaction within *The Times Good University Guide 2015*, the *Complete University Guide 2016* and *The Guardian University Guide 2016*. The latter focuses particularly on student satisfaction and in this it was ranked 6th in the UK for student satisfaction with assessment and feedback, ahead of all Russell Group universities.

The story since the granting of University status in 2005 provides powerful evidence of the institution's success in cementing its position as a key participant in the city of Chester, the Borough of Warrington, Cheshire and the Wirral, a major force locally in educational provision in the North West of England and increasingly at national and international levels. Its phenomenal growth in terms of student numbers, new buildings and the variety in the curricula offered, would have astounded those first students attending classes in the 'somewhat gloomy' house in Nicholas Street in the early years of Queen Victoria's reign, and long gone are the days when a key strategy document like the 1923 Deeside Regional Planning Scheme could be written without mentioning Chester College.

It is also premature and, to a degree presumptuous, to attempt an overview of the era of the present Vice-Chancellor. Yet, it is not unreasonable to predict that, in any future assessment of the long story of the institution, Timothy Wheeler's name will stand alongside those of the Founders amongst those who have done

Above: Celebrating the Chester Students' Union success as top in the North West for student satisfaction

Above: Professor Anna Sutton

Foundational Values 2015

Mindful of the University's history and Christian foundation:

We recognise the dignity and worth of every individual.

Therefore we value every member of the University;

we endeavour to help each student and member of staff to discover

his or her gifts and talents and grow to full potential;

and we foster well-being for all.

We recognise the vital role of education in the service of society.

Therefore we encourage the acquisition of knowledge

and the development of skills;

and we acknowledge a responsibility to look for every opportunity to put that

knowledge and those skills to good use throughout the community.

We recognise the inherent value of the pursuit of truth and freedom of enquiry.

Therefore we find joy in discovery;

we take pleasure in invention;

we celebrate human creativity;

and we seek wisdom, embracing it wherever we find it

and strive to apply it to every aspect of life.

In humility, we aspire to honour these values and hold ourselves accountable to them.

most to shape its history. In bringing the University into being and expanding its size, influence, breadth of curriculum and reputation in so short a time, he has decisively made Chester the University city which many wished for decades ago. In a recent interview with the author he modestly pointed to the contribution of his colleagues and said 'many opportunities have by good luck fallen into my lap', to which the obvious reply is 'but they need a receptive and prepared lap to fall into'. Like his successful predecessors he has been the right man at the right time.

It is, of course, highly artificial to compare the major University of 2015 with the original 'seminary for the training of masters' of 1839. Yet it is perhaps justified in an overview spanning 176 years, to contrast, for example, the 26 students of 1841 and a permanent staff of two, with the 19,000 students of 2015 and a staff of 1,897. As late as 1953, when our present Queen was crowned, there were only 151 students and an academic staff of 12.

The University retains a distinct identity, notably from its leading role amongst The Cathedrals Group of Universities. The 2013 Annual Report concentrated rightly on the 'Chester Difference', not least upon the distinctive and personalised experience available to Chester students.

A current indication of the University's significance is the fact that it makes a contribution of more than £400million per annum to the region, according to the latest independent economic impact assessment report.

Above: The University of Chester rose commissioned to commemorate the 175th anniversary

Below: The Riverside Campus in Chester at the bottom centre of the picture, based in the former County Hall with the Queen's Park Campus on the south bank, top centre

The values and ethos of service that were so supremely important to its Founders remain central to the University's success as it continues to respond to the demands of an ever more rapidly changing society.

Revisiting the prophetic words of Mr Gladstone at the opening of the new College building in 1842, former students can now 'be found imparting to others the knowledge they had acquired ... in Chester', not merely 'to the people of these realms', but to those of other parts of the world.

The 'bright star' that is the University of Chester continues both to shine and increase in magnitude.

Left: The 2015 Cathedrals Group Choirs' Festival in Chester Cathedral

Left: Watercolour of the 175th anniversary procession by alumnus Thomas Plunkett, who studied Fine Art under John Renshaw at Chester College and is currently President of the Royal Watercolour Society

Above: Etching of 'Old College' by Ronald Basil Emsley Woodhouse, *c.*1924

Above: Professor Graeme White with *On Chester On*, the definitive history of the University, published by the University of Chester Press in 2014

Acknowledgements and Sources

Anyone dealing with the early history of Chester College in a chronological way must acknowledge a substantial debt to John L. Bradbury's *Chester College and the Training of Teachers*, published by the Governors in 1975. *The Victoria History of the County of Chester*, Vol. V, Part 2 (2005) includes, in the chapter on 'Education' by Malcolm Seaborne (pp. 277 ff.), an admirably concise account of the College, extended to modern times, and my thanks are due to Dr Alan Thacker, Executive Editor, and the University of London for permission to make free use of this material. More thematic material has been culled from *Perspectives of Chester College: 150th Anniversary Essays, 1839–1989*, edited by Professor Graeme White in 1989. The new *Oxford Dictionary of National Biography* (Oxford, 2004) contains biographies of all six Founders, Sir William Crookes and of Sir Bernard de Bunsen.

Most importantly, readers now have the benefit of Professor Graeme J. White's meticulously researched, analytical and definitive account. *On Chester On: A History of Chester College and the University of Chester* which was published by the University of Chester Press in 2014 and I am deeply grateful to him for readily allowing use of his research in updating and enhancing this present edition.

The University of Chester's own archives, however, provide the bulk of what is retold here and I am grateful to Mrs Diana Dunn, Hon. University Archivist and to the former County Archivist, Mr Jonathan Pepler, and Cheshire Archives and Local Studies for free access to the collection. Particular thanks are due to Mr Derek Joinson and Mr Adam Kinnersley of Cheshire Archives and Local Studies for their pains in facilitating this access and to Mr Brett Langston for help with the detective work in correcting the often repeated, but erroneous, identification of the temporary premises in Nicholas Street occupied by the College from 1840 to 1842.

All illustrations, except those specifically mentioned below, are taken from the archives and collections of the University. Special thanks are due to Mr Matthew Perrin of the University's Learning Resources Department for his expert photography of the archive material. The three most recent principals have read and commented on the sections dealing with their respective eras. The modern section could not have been written without the expert help of Professors Glyn Turton and Graeme White, and Dr Sarah Griffiths, co-ordinator of the excellently produced Annual Reviews. The advice of Mrs Diana Dunn, former Senior Lecturer in History and Director of Undergraduate Programmes, has been indispensable throughout and especially in picture research.

For expert production of this book, the credit must go to Sarah Griffiths, Managing Editor of the University of Chester Press, and to the designers, Ms Elpiniki Vavritsa, Mr Matthew Houghton, Mrs Diane Dennis and Mr Gary Martin. My unbounded gratitude also goes to Mrs Alison Turner and Mrs Lynn McCrimmon of the former Cheshire County Council for typing the original manuscript. The attention to detail by all these people has been beyond praise.

Specific thanks and permissions to reproduce illustrations are as follows:

- The Chapter of Chester Cathedral and Cheshire Archives and Local Studies for the portraits of Bishop Sumner, Henry Raikes, Canon Slade, Dean Anson and Dean Bennett.
- Cheshire County Council and Cheshire Archives and Local Studies for the Romney view of the College from the west of 1842 (on the title page) for newspaper extracts (by permission of Trinity Mirror Cheshire) and for the 1830s print of Bridge House.
- The Flintshire Record Office for the 1839 portrait of W.E. Gladstone.
- Warrington Borough Council's Library, Museum and Archives Service (through the efforts of Ms Jo Unsworth and Mrs Hilary Chambers) for the portrait of Horatio Powys and the view of the Warrington National School.
- The Chester History and Heritage Centre for the photograph of the demolished premises in Nicholas Street, recorded by the Chester Photographic Survey.
- Parry's *Panorama* (1843), the panoramic view of Chester reproduced on p. 2, and the R.K. Thomas lithograph showing the new Chapel (*c.*1846) are from private collections.
- Mrs. Sue Benson of Cheshire County Council for the photograph of the garden front of Bridge House.
- Mr David Hooper for the cricketing picture on p. 19.
- The photograph of Principal Ned Binks on p. 34 is copyright of Guardian Newspapers Ltd, 1992.

My final expression of gratitude must go to Professor Timothy Wheeler, Vice-Chancellor of the University of Chester, and to Mr Jeremy Taylor, Former Chief Executive of Cheshire County Council, for their original encouragement to produce this book.

The original edition of 2005 was updated to 2008 for the second edition by Mr Peter Williams. This has in turn been updated and amended by Ian Dunn with the indispensable help of Sarah Griffiths for the subsequent editions.